KETO DIET

Cookbook for Beginners 2024

2000 Days Delicious Recipes, Stress-free 30-Day
Keto Diet Planner with Low Carb to Lose Weight

Sharon J. Morris

CONTENTS

THE BEST KETO SNACKS

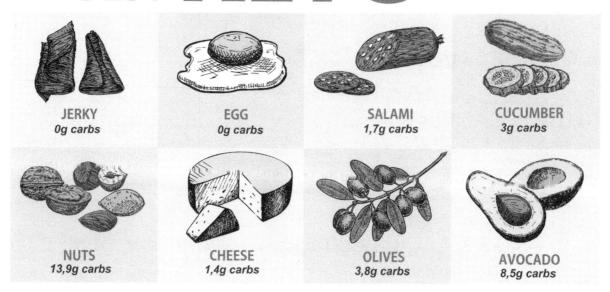

JERKY 0g carbs	**EGG** 0g carbs	**SALAMI** 1,7g carbs	**CUCUMBER** 3g carbs
NUTS 13,9g carbs	**CHEESE** 1,4g carbs	**OLIVES** 3,8g carbs	**AVOCADO** 8,5g carbs

Homemade
COOKING

INTRODUCTION

Sharon J. Morris is a dedicated nutritionist, culinary enthusiast, and wellness advocate, renowned for her passion for creating delicious, health-conscious recipes. With over a decade of experience in the field of nutrition and a deep-rooted commitment to helping individuals achieve their wellness goals, Sharon has become a trusted source of guidance and inspiration in the world of healthy living.

The process of writing her acclaimed book, "The Keto Diet Cookbook," was a labor of love that combined her extensive knowledge with her newfound passion for ketogenic cuisine. Sharon's meticulous approach involved in-depth research on the science behind ketosis, as well as the creative process of developing mouthwatering, keto-friendly recipes. Her goal was not just to provide a cookbook but to craft a comprehensive guide that would empower readers to embrace a ketogenic lifestyle confidently.

As an author, Sharon's dedication to her craft shines through in the meticulous detail she brings to every page of "The Keto Diet Cookbook." Her recipes are not only delicious but also nutritionally balanced, making them suitable for both beginners and seasoned keto enthusiasts. Sharon's warm and encouraging voice throughout the book makes the journey to keto not only accessible but also enjoyable.

"The Keto Diet Cookbook" is not just a cookbook; it is a testament to Sharon's unwavering commitment to improving the lives of others through the power of delicious, nutritious food. With her expertise and passion, she invites you to embark on your own transformative journey towards a healthier, happier you.

What is the keto diet? Why is it so popular?

The ketogenic diet, often referred to as the keto diet, is a low-carb, high-fat diet that has gained huge popularity in recent years. It is designed to encourage the body to enter a state known as ketosis, in which the body burns primarily fat rather than carbohydrates for fuel

Key principles of the keto diet:

- Low carbohydrate intake

- High fat intake

- Moderate amounts of protein

- Ketosis: The purpose of the diet is to induce a metabolic state known as ketosis. In a state of ketosis, the body shifts from primarily utilizing glucose (from carbohydrates) as a source of energy to utilizing ketone bodies, which are molecules produced by the breakdown of fat. This process promotes fat burning for energy, which leads to weight loss.

So, why is the keto diet so popular?

Effective Weight Loss: Many people turn to the keto diet because it has been shown to be effective for weight loss. By shifting the body into ketosis, it can lead to rapid fat loss, which can be appealing for those seeking to shed excess pounds.

Improved Blood Sugar Control: The keto diet may help stabilize blood sugar levels, making it appealing to individuals with diabetes or those looking to manage their insulin resistance.

Reduced Hunger: Some individuals find that the keto diet helps them feel full and satisfied for longer periods due to the increased fat intake. This can make it easier to control calorie intake and reduce snacking.

What You Can and Can't Eat on the Keto Diet

 Keto Diet

Foods You Can Eat on the Keto Diet:

1. **Healthy Fats:** These are the foundation of the keto diet, providing the majority of your daily calories.

Avocados   Olive oil   Coconut oil   Butter and ghee (clarified butter)   Nuts and seeds (in moderation) Fatty cuts of meat (e.g., salmon, bacon)

2. **Protein Sources:** Choose lean and fatty protein sources, but be mindful of portion sizes.

Chicken   Turkey   Beef   Pork   Fish (especially fatty fish like salmon)

Eggs   Dairy products (e.g., cheese, yogurt)

3. **Non-Starchy Vegetables:** These are low in carbohydrates and can be consumed in moderate amounts.

Leafy greens (e.g., spinach, kale, lettuce)   Broccoli Cauliflower   Zucchini   Bell peppers   Tomatoes (in moderation)

4. **Low-Carb Fruits (in moderation):** Some fruits are lower in carbohydrates and can be consumed in limited quantities.

Berries (e.g., strawberries, blueberries, raspberries)

5. **Beverages:** Water and sparkling water   Unsweetened tea and coffee   Herbal tea   Sugar-free, unsweetened almond milk

Foods You Can't Eat on the Keto Diet:

1. **High-Carb Foods:** Avoid or strictly limit foods that are high in carbohydrates.

Sugar (all forms, including table sugar, honey, and maple syrup)

Grains (e.g., wheat, rice, oats)

Starchy vegetables (e.g., potatoes, corn)

Legumes (e.g., beans, lentils)

Most fruits (due to their high sugar content)

Processed foods (e.g., sugary snacks, chips)

2. **Sugary Beverages:** Soda (both regular and diet) Fruit juices   Sweetened tea and coffee

3. **Processed Carbohydrates:** White bread   Pasta Cereals   Cakes, cookies, and pastries   Candy and sweets

Chips and crackers

4. **Alcohol (in moderation):** Some alcoholic beverages are high in carbohydrates.

Beer (typically high in carbs)   Sweet cocktails

5. **Unhealthy Fats:** Avoid trans fats and highly processed vegetable oils.

Trans fats (e.g., margarine)   Highly processed vegetable oils (e.g., corn and soybean oil)

6 Things I Wish You Knew Before You Started Living the Keto Diet

Before embarking on the keto diet, it's crucial to have a clear understanding of its principles and potential effects on your body.

● **Understanding Ketosis:**

Keto is short for "ketogenic," which refers to a metabolic state called ketosis. In ketosis, your body primarily uses fat for energy instead of carbohydrates. To achieve ketosis, you must significantly reduce your carb intake and increase your fat consumption.

● **Carbohydrate Restriction:**

The keto diet is extremely low in carbohydrates. You'll typically aim to consume no more than 20-50 grams of carbs per day, depending on individual factors. This restriction helps trigger ketosis.

● **Importance of Fats:**

Healthy fats become the primary source of energy on the keto diet. You'll need to embrace foods rich in healthy fats like avocados, olive oil, nuts, seeds, and fatty cuts of meat.

● **Moderate Protein Intake:**

Protein intake on the keto diet should be moderate. Consuming too much protein can potentially interfere with ketosis, as excess protein can be converted into glucose. Aim for an appropriate balance between fats and protein.

● **Possible Side Effects (Keto Flu):**

When transitioning to keto, some people experience side effects known as the "keto flu." Symptoms may include fatigue, headache, nausea, and irritability. These usually subside within a few days to a week as your body adapts.

● **Hydration and Electrolytes:**

Ketosis can lead to increased water loss and a loss of electrolytes (sodium, potassium, magnesium). It's essential to stay well-hydrated and consider adding electrolyte-rich foods or supplements to your diet to prevent imbalances.

Reasons to Recommend the Keto Diet Cookbook

Variety and Inspiration: A ketogenic diet can become repetitive without creative recipes. A recipe book provides a wide range of ideas and cooking techniques to keep meals exciting and satisfying.

Nutrient Balance: A well-crafted ketogenic recipe book can help ensure that you maintain the right balance of macronutrients (fats, proteins, and carbohydrates) necessary for the keto diet, preventing overconsumption of carbs and promoting ketosis.

Meal Planning: Recipe books often include meal plans and grocery lists, making it easier to plan your keto meals for the week. This can save time and reduce the stress of meal preparation.

Educational Value: Many recipe books include educational sections that explain the principles of the ketogenic diet, helping readers understand why certain foods are included and how they affect the body.

Portion Control: Recipes in a book are usually portioned out, helping you control your calorie intake and adhere to the keto diet's guidelines.

Avoiding Common Pitfalls: Keto diet recipe books often offer tips and tricks to avoid common pitfalls that people encounter while following the diet, such as hidden carbs or inadequate fat intake.

Weight Loss Support: For those using the keto diet for weight loss, a recipe book can be a valuable tool to help track calorie and nutrient intake while enjoying flavorful meals.

Health Benefits: The ketogenic diet has been associated with various health benefits, such as improved blood sugar control, increased energy, and potential weight loss. A recipe book tailored to this diet can assist in achieving these goals.

Diverse Cuisine: Many ketogenic recipe books offer a variety of cuisines, from Mediterranean to Asian, allowing individuals to enjoy their favorite flavors while staying in ketosis.

KETO > **BREAKFAST**

KETO > **LUNCH**

KETO > **DINNER**

30 Day Meal Plan

DAY	BREAKFAST	LUNCH	DINNER
1	French Fried Butternut Squash 13	Asparagus Niçoise Salad 51	Beefy Scotch Eggs 25
2	Asian Glazed Meatballs 13	Tuna Salad With Lettuce & Olives 51	Pork Nachos 25
3	Cheesy Cauliflower Fritters 14	Chicken And Cauliflower Rice Soup 51	Juicy Pork Medallions 25
4	Crispy Keto Pork Bites 14	Citrusy Brussels Sprouts Salad 51	Simple Corned Beef 25
5	Crab Stuffed Mushrooms 15	Green Salad 52	Beef Meatballs With Onion Sauce 26
6	Air Fryer Garlic Chicken Wings 15	Broccoli Slaw Salad With Mustard-mayo Dressing 52	Slow-cooked Beef Moroccan Style 26
7	Chocolate Mousse 16	Cobb Egg Salad In Lettuce Cups 52	Beef Cheeseburger Casserole 26
8	Grilled Cheese Bacon Jalapeno 16	Thyme & Wild Mushroom Soup 53	Jalapeno Beef Pot Roasted 27
9	Bacon Mashed Cauliflower 15	Pumpkin & Meat Peanut Stew 53	Ribeye Steak With Shitake Mushrooms 28
10	Roasted Cauliflower With Serrano Ham & Pine Nuts 16	Fruit Salad With Poppy Seeds 53	Beef And Ale Pot Roast 27
11	Turkey Pastrami & Mascarpone Cheese Pinwheels 17	Caesar Salad With Smoked Salmon And Poached Eggs 53	Hot Pork With Dill Pickles 28
12	Easy Garlic Keto Bread 17	Spinach Fruit Salad With Seeds 54	Caribbean Beef 28
13	Soy Garlic Mushrooms 18	Cream Of Thyme Tomato Soup 54	Rib Roast With Roasted Red Shallots And Garlic 27
14	Squid Salad With Mint, Cucumber & Chili Dressing 17	Chicken Cabbage Soup 55	Smoked Pork Sausages With Mushrooms 28
15	Coconut Ginger Macaroons 18	Creamy Soup With Greens 54	Pork Lettuce Cups 29

DAY	BREAKFAST	LUNCH	DINNER
16	Basil Keto Crackers 18	Watermelon And Cucumber Salad 55	Spicy Pork Stew With Spinach 29
17	Walnut Butter On Cracker 17	Bacon And Spinach Salad 55	Beef Sausage Casserole 29
18	Zesty Balsamic Chard 18	Mushroom-broccoli Soup 55	Keto Beefy Burritos 29
19	Cardamom And Cinnamon Fat Bombs 19	Bacon Chowder 56	Lettuce Taco Carnitas 30
20	Mascarpone Snapped Amaretti Biscuits 19	Kale And Brussels Sprouts 56	Garlic Pork Chops With Mint Pesto 30
21	Parsnip And Carrot Fries With Aioli 19	Mushroom Soup 56	Dr. Pepper Pulled Pork 30
22	Ricotta And Pomegranate 20	Pesto Tomato Cucumber Salad 56	Peanut Butter Pork Stir-fry 31
23	Party Bacon And Pistachio Balls 20	Easy Tomato Salad 57	Balsamic Grilled Pork Chops 31
24	Apricot And Soy Nut Trail Mix 21	Beef Reuben Soup 57	Pork Goulash With Cauliflower 31
25	Garlicky Cheddar Biscuits 21	Spicy Chicken Bean Soup 57	Beef Stovies 31
26	Devilled Eggs With Sriracha Mayo 21	Green Mackerel Salad 58	Mustardy Pork Chops 32
27	Parmesan Crackers 22	Insalata Caprese 57	Baked Pork Meatballs In Pasta Sauce 32
28	Buttery Herb Roasted Radishes 22	Brazilian Moqueca (shrimp Stew) 58	Garlic Crispy Pork Loin 32
29	Cocoa Nuts Goji Bars 22	Creamy Cauliflower Soup With Chorizo Sausage 58	Cocoa-crusted Pork Tenderloin 33
30	Italian-style Chicken Wraps 23	Broccoli Cheese Soup 59	Seasoned Garlic Pork Chops 33

Appetizers, Snacks & Side Dishes Recipes

Appetizers, Snacks & Side Dishes Recipes

Roasted Stuffed Piquillo Peppers

Servings: 8
Cooking Time: 20 Minutes

Ingredients:
- 8 canned roasted piquillo peppers
- 1 tbsp olive oil
- 3 slices prosciutto, cut into thin slices
- 1 tbsp balsamic vinegar
- Filling:
- 8 ounces goat cheese
- 3 tbsp heavy cream
- 3 tbsp chopped parsley
- ½ tsp minced garlic
- 1 tbsp olive oil
- 1 tbsp chopped mint

Directions:
1. Mix all filling ingredients in a bowl. Place in a freezer bag, press down and squeeze, and cut off the bottom. Drain and deseed the peppers. Squeeze about 2 tbsp of the filling into each pepper.
2. Wrap a prosciutto slice onto each pepper. Secure with toothpicks. Arrange them on a serving platter. Sprinkle the olive oil and vinegar over.

Nutrition Info:
- Per Servings 2.5g Carbs, 6g Protein, 11g Fat, 132 Calories

French Fried Butternut Squash

Servings: 6
Cooking Time: 20 Minutes

Ingredients:
- 1 medium butternut squash
- 1 tablespoon chopped fresh thyme
- 1 tablespoon chopped fresh rosemary
- 4 tablespoons olive oil
- 1/2 teaspoon salt
- Cooking spray

Directions:
1. Heat oven to 425oF. Lightly coat a baking sheet with cooking spray.
2. Peel skin from butternut squash and cut into even sticks, about 1/2-inch-wide and 3 inches long.
3. In a medium bowl, combine the squash, oil, thyme, rosemary, and salt; mix until the squash is evenly coated.
4. Spread onto the baking sheet and roast for 10 minutes.
5. Remove the baking sheet from the oven and shake to loosen the squash.
6. Return to oven and continue to roast for 10 minutes or until golden brown.
7. Serve and enjoy.

Nutrition Info:
- Per Servings 1g Carbs, 1g Protein, 9g Fat, 86 Calories

Asian Glazed Meatballs

Servings: 4
Cooking Time: 35 Minutes

Ingredients:
- 1-pound frozen meatballs, thawed to room temperature
- ½ cup hoisin sauce
- 1 tablespoon apricot jam
- 2 tablespoons soy sauce
- ½ teaspoon sesame oil
- 5 tbsp MCT oil or coconut oil
- 2 tbsp water

Directions:
1. Place a heavy-bottomed pot on medium-high fire and heat coconut oil.
2. Sauté meatballs until lightly browned, around 10 minutes.
3. Stir in remaining ingredients and mix well.
4. Cover and cook for 25 minutes on low fire, mixing now and then.
5. Serve and enjoy.

Nutrition Info:
- Per Servings 6.5g Carbs, 16.3g Protein, 51.6g Fat, 536 Calories

Nutty Avocado Crostini With Nori

Servings: 4

Cooking Time: 12 Minutes

Ingredients:
- 8 slices low carb baguette
- 4 nori sheets
- 1 cup mashed avocado
- ⅓ tsp salt
- 1 tsp lemon juice
- 1 ½ tbsp coconut oil
- ⅓ cup chopped raw walnuts
- 1 tbsp chia seeds

Directions:

1. In a bowl, flake the nori sheets into the smallest possible pieces.

2. In another bowl, mix the avocado, salt, and lemon juice, and stir in half of the nori flakes. Set aside.

3. Place the baguette on a baking sheet and toast in a broiler on medium heat for 2 minutes, making sure not to burn. Remove the crostini after and brush with coconut oil on both sides.

4. Top each crostini with the avocado mixture and garnish with the chia seeds, chopped walnuts, Serve the snack immediately.

Nutrition Info:
- Per Servings 2.8g Carbs, 13.7g Protein, 12.2g Fat, 195 Calories

Cheesy Cauliflower Fritters

Servings: 4

Cooking Time: 35 Minutes

Ingredients:
- 1 pound grated cauliflower
- ½ cup Parmesan cheese
- 3 ounces chopped onion
- ½ tsp baking powder
- ½ cup almond flour
- 3 eggs
- ½ tsp lemon juice
- 2 tbsp olive oil
- ⅓ tsp salt

Directions:

1. Sprinkle the salt over the cauliflower in a bowl, and let it stand for 10 minutes. Add in the other ingredients. Mix with your hands to combine. Place a skillet over medium heat, and heat olive oil.

2. Shape fritters out of the cauliflower mixture. Fry in batches, for about 3 minutes per side.

Nutrition Info:
- Per Servings 3g Carbs, 4.5g Protein, 4.5g Fat, 69 Calories

Shrimp Fra Diavolo

Servings: 3

Cooking Time: 5 Minutes

Ingredients:
- 3 tablespoons butter
- 1 onion, diced
- 5 cloves of garlic, minced
- 1 teaspoon red pepper flakes
- ¼ pound shrimps, shelled
- 2 tablespoons olive oil
- Salt and pepper to taste

Directions:

1. Heat the butter and the olive oil in a skillet and sauté the onion and garlic until fragrant.

2. Stir in the red pepper flakes and shrimps. Season with salt and pepper to taste.

3. Stir for 3 minutes.

4. Serve and enjoy.

Nutrition Info:
- Per Servings 4.5g Carbs, 21.0g Protein, 32.1g Fat, 388 Calories

Crispy Keto Pork Bites

Servings: 3

Cooking Time: 30 Minutes

Ingredients:
- ½ pork belly, sliced to thin strips
- 1 tablespoon butter
- 1 onion, diced
- 4 tablespoons coconut cream
- Salt and pepper to taste

Directions:

1. Place all ingredients in a mixing bowl and allow to marinate in the fridge for 2 hours.

2. When 2 hours is nearly up, preheat oven to 400oF and lightly grease a cookie sheet with cooking spray.

3. Place the pork strips in an even layer on the cookie sheet.

4. Roast for 30 minutes and turnover halfway through cooking.

Nutrition Info:
- Per Servings 1.9g Carbs, 19.1g Protein, 40.6g Fat, 448 Calories

Crab Stuffed Mushrooms

Servings: 3
Cooking Time: 25 Minutes

Ingredients:
- 2 tbsp minced green onion
- 1 cup cooked crabmeat, chopped finely
- ¼ cup Monterey Jack cheese, shredded
- 1 tsp lemon juice
- ¼ lb, fresh button mushrooms
- Pepper and salt to taste
- 3 tablespoons olive oil

Directions:
1. Destem mushrooms, wash, and drain well.
2. Chop mushroom stems.
3. Preheat oven to 400oF and lightly grease a baking pan with cooking spray.
4. In a small bowl, whisk well green onion, crabmeat, lemon juice, dill, and chopped mushroom stems.
5. Evenly spread mushrooms on prepared pan with cap sides up. Evenly spoon crabmeat mixture on top of mushroom caps.
6. Pop in the oven and bake for 20 minutes.
7. Remove from oven and sprinkle cheese on top.
8. Return to oven and broil for 3 minutes.
9. Serve and enjoy.

Nutrition Info:
- Per Servings 10g Carbs, 7.9g Protein, 17.3g Fat, 286 Calories

Air Fryer Garlic Chicken Wings

Servings: 4
Cooking Time: 25 Minutes

Ingredients:
- 16 pieces chicken wings
- ¾ cup almond flour
- 4 tablespoons minced garlic
- ¼ cup butter, melted
- 2 tablespoons Stevia powder
- Salt and pepper to taste

Directions:
1. Preheat oven to 400oF.
2. In a mixing bowl, combine the chicken wings, almond flour, Stevia powder, and garlic. Season with salt and pepper to taste.
3. Place in a lightly greased cookie sheet in an even layer and cook for 25 minutes.
4. Halfway through the cooking time, turnover chicken.

5. Once cooked, place in a bowl and drizzle with melted butter. Toss to coat.
6. Serve and enjoy.

Nutrition Info:
- Per Servings 7.8g Carbs, 23.7g Protein, 26.9g Fat, 365 Calories

Bacon Mashed Cauliflower

Servings: 6
Cooking Time: 40 Minutes

Ingredients:
- 6 slices bacon
- 3 heads cauliflower, leaves removed
- 2 cups water
- 2 tbsp melted butter
- ½ cup buttermilk
- Salt and black pepper to taste
- ¼ cup grated yellow cheddar cheese
- 2 tbsp chopped chives

Directions:
1. Preheat oven to 350ºF. Fry bacon in a heated skillet over medium heat for 5 minutes until crispy. Remove to a paper towel-lined plate, allow to cool, and crumble. Set aside and keep bacon fat.
2. Boil cauli heads in water in a pot over high heat for 7 minutes, until tender. Drain and put in a bowl.
3. Include butter, buttermilk, salt, black pepper, and puree using a hand blender until smooth and creamy. Lightly grease a casserole dish with the bacon fat and spread the mash in it.
4. Sprinkle with cheddar cheese and place under the broiler for 4 minutes on high until the cheese melts. Remove and top with bacon and chopped chives. Serve with pan-seared scallops.

Nutrition Info:
- Per Servings 6g Carbs, 14g Protein, 25g Fat, 312 Calories

Grilled Cheese Bacon Jalapeno

Servings: 2
Cooking Time: 40 Mins

Ingredients:
- 8 ounces cream cheese
- 2 tablespoons grated Parmesan cheese
- 1 1/2 cups shredded Cheddar cheese
- 16 whole jalapeno peppers with stems
- 8 slices bacon, cut in half crosswise
- Oil spray
- 1 1/2 teaspoons garlic powder

Directions:
1. Preheat a grill over medium heat and brush grill grates with oil.
2. Combine cream cheese, Parmesan cheese, cheddar cheese and garlic powder in a small bowl, toss well.
3. Cut the jalapeños in half lengthwise. Using a small spoon, scrape out seeds & membranes.
4. Stuff the cheese mixture into the jalapeno halves. Wrap each jalapeno completely with bacon. Secure with toothpicks.
5. Place jalapenos on the grill and grill until cheese mixture is hot and bubbling around the edges, about 30 to 40 minutes.

Nutrition Info:
- Per Servings 1.6g Carbs, 5.8g Protein, 15g Fat, 164 Calories

Chocolate Mousse

Servings: 4
Cooking Time: 0 Minutes

Ingredients:
- 1 large, ripe avocado
- 1/4 cup sweetened almond milk
- 1 tbsp coconut oil
- 1/4 cup cocoa or cacao powder
- 1 tsp vanilla extract

Directions:
1. In a food processor, process all ingredients until smooth and creamy.
2. Transfer to a lidded container and chill for at least 4 hours.
3. Serve and enjoy.

Nutrition Info:
- Per Servings 6.9g Carbs, 1.2g Protein, 11.0g Fat, 125 Calories

Lemony Fried Artichokes

Servings: 4
Cooking Time: 20 Minutes

Ingredients:
- 12 fresh baby artichokes
- 2 tbsp lemon juice
- 2 tbsp olive oil
- Salt to taste

Directions:
1. Slice the artichokes vertically into narrow wedges. Drain on paper towels before frying.
2. Heat olive oil in a cast-iron skillet over high heat. Fry the artichokes until browned and crispy. Drain excess oil on paper towels. Sprinkle with salt and lemon juice.

Nutrition Info:
- Per Servings 2.9g Carbs, 2g Protein, 2.4g Fat, 35 Calories

Roasted Cauliflower With Serrano Ham & Pine Nuts

Servings: 6
Cooking Time: 30 Minutes

Ingredients:
- 2 heads cauliflower, cut into 1-inch slices
- 2 tbsp olive oil
- Salt and chili pepper to taste
- 1 tsp garlic powder
- 10 slices Serrano ham, chopped
- ¼ cup pine nuts, chopped
- 1 tsp capers
- 1 tsp parsley

Directions:
1. Preheat oven to 450ºF and line a baking sheet with foil.
2. Brush the cauli steaks with olive oil and season with chili pepper, garlic, and salt.
3. Spread the cauli florets on the baking sheet. Roast in the oven for 10 minutes until tender and lightly browned. Remove the sheet and sprinkle the ham and pine nuts all over the cauli. Bake for another 10 minutes until the ham is crispy and a nutty aroma is perceived.
4. Take out, sprinkle with capers and parsley. Serve with ground beef stew and braised asparagus.

Nutrition Info:
- Per Servings 2.5g Carbs, 10g Protein, 10g Fat, 141 Calories

Turkey Pastrami & Mascarpone Cheese Pinwheels

Servings: 4
Cooking Time: 40 Minutes

Ingredients:
- Cooking spray
- 8 oz mascarpone cheese
- 10 oz turkey pastrami, sliced
- 10 canned pepperoncini peppers, sliced and drained

Directions:

1. Lay a 12 x 12 plastic wrap on a flat surface and arrange the pastrami all over slightly overlapping each other. Spread the cheese on top of the salami layers and arrange the pepperoncini on top.

2. Hold two opposite ends of the plastic wrap and roll the pastrami. Twist both ends to tighten and refrigerate for 2 hours. Unwrap the salami roll and slice into 2-inch pinwheels. Serve.

Nutrition Info:
- Per Servings 0g Carbs, 13g Protein, 24g Fat, 266 Calories

Squid Salad With Mint, Cucumber & Chili Dressing

Servings: 4
Cooking Time: 30 Minutes

Ingredients:
- 4 medium squid tubes, cut into strips
- ½ cup mint leaves
- 2 medium cucumbers, halved and cut in strips
- ½ cup coriander leaves, reserve the stems
- ½ red onion, finely sliced
- Salt and black pepper to taste
- 1 tsp fish sauce
- 1 red chili, roughly chopped
- 1 tsp swerve
- 1 clove garlic
- 2 limes, juiced
- 1 tbsp chopped coriander
- 1tsp olive oil

Directions:

1. In a salad bowl, mix mint leaves, cucumber strips, coriander leaves, and red onion. Season with salt, pepper and a little drizzle of olive oil; set aside. In the mortar, pound the coriander stems, red chili, and swerve into a paste using the pestle. Add the fish sauce and lime juice, and mix with the pestle.

2. Heat a skillet over high heat on a stovetop and sear the squid on both sides to lightly brown, about 5 minutes. Pour the squid on the salad and drizzle with the chili dressing. Toss the ingredients with two spoons, garnish with coriander, and serve the salad as a single dish or with some more seafood.

Nutrition Info:
- Per Servings 2.1g Carbs, 24.6g Protein, 22.5g Fat, 318 Calories

Easy Garlic Keto Bread

Servings: 1
Cooking Time: 1 Minute 30 Seconds

Ingredients:
- 1 large egg
- 1 tbsp milk
- 1 tbsp coconut flour
- 1 tbsp almond flour
- ¼ tsp baking powder
- Salt to taste

Directions:

1. Mix all ingredients in a bowl until well combined.
2. Pour into a mug and place in the microwave oven.
3. Cook for 1 minute and 30 seconds.
4. Once cooked, invert the mug.
5. Allow to cool before slicing.

Nutrition Info:
- Per Servings 3g Carbs, 4g Protein, 7g Fat, 75 Calories

Walnut Butter On Cracker

Servings: 1
Cooking Time: 0 Minutes

Ingredients:
- 1 tablespoon walnut butter
- 2 pieces Mary's gone crackers

Directions:

1. Spread ½ tablespoon of walnut butter per cracker and enjoy.

Nutrition Info:
- Per Servings 4.0g Carbs, 1.0g Protein, 14.0g Fat, 134 Calories

Soy Garlic Mushrooms

Servings: 8
Cooking Time: 10 Minutes

Ingredients:
- 2 pounds mushrooms, sliced
- 3 tablespoons olive oil
- 2 cloves of garlic, minced
- ¼ cup coconut aminos
- 4 tablespoons butter
- Salt and pepper to taste

Directions:
1. Place all ingredients in a dish except for the butter and mix until well-combined.
2. Allow marinating for 2 hours in the fridge.
3. In a large saucepan on medium fire, melt the butter and add mushrooms and sauté for 8 minutes. Season with pepper and salt to taste.
4. Serve and enjoy.

Nutrition Info:
- Per Servings 4.7g Carbs, 3.8g Protein, 11.9g Fat, 152 Calories

Coconut Ginger Macaroons

Servings: 6
Cooking Time: 20 Minutes

Ingredients:
- 2 fingers ginger root, peeled and pureed
- 6 egg whites
- 1 cup finely shredded coconut
- ¼ cup swerve
- A pinch of chili powder
- 1 cup water
- Angel hair chili to garnish

Directions:
1. Preheat the oven to 350ºF and line a baking sheet with parchment paper. Set aside.
2. Then, in a heatproof bowl, whisk the ginger, egg whites, shredded coconut, swerve, and chili powder.
3. Bring the water to boil in a pot over medium heat and place the heatproof bowl on the pot. Then, continue whisking the mixture until it is glossy, about 4 minutes. Do not let the bowl touch the water or be too hot so that the eggs don't cook.
4. Spoon the mixture into the piping bag after and pipe out 40 to 50 little mounds on the lined baking sheet. Bake the macaroons in the middle part of the oven for 15 minutes.
5. Once they are ready, transfer them to a wire rack,

garnish them with the angel hair chili, and serve.

Nutrition Info:
- Per Servings 0.3g Carbs, 6.8g Protein, 3.5g Fat, 97 Calories

Basil Keto Crackers

Servings: 6
Cooking Time: 15 Minutes

Ingredients:
- 1 ¼ cups almond flour
- ½ teaspoon baking powder
- ¼ teaspoon dried basil powder
- A pinch of cayenne pepper powder
- 1 clove of garlic, minced
- What you'll need from the store cupboard:
- Salt and pepper to taste
- 3 tablespoons oil

Directions:
1. Preheat oven to 350oF and lightly grease a cookie sheet with cooking spray.
2. Mix everything in a mixing bowl to create a dough.
3. Transfer the dough on a clean and flat working surface and spread out until 2mm thick. Cut into squares.
4. Place gently in an even layer on the prepped cookie sheet. Cook for 10 minutes.
5. Cook in batches.
6. Serve and enjoy.

Nutrition Info:
- Per Servings 2.9g Carbs, 5.3g Protein, 19.3g Fat, 205 Calories

Zesty Balsamic Chard

Servings: 6
Cooking Time: 20 Minutes

Ingredients:
- 2 medium onions, chopped
- 6 garlic cloves, sliced
- 1/2 cup white balsamic vinegar
- 2 bunches Swiss chard, coarsely chopped
- 1/2 cup walnut halves, toasted
- 1/4 teaspoon salt
- 1/4 teaspoon pepper
- 3 tablespoons olive oil

Directions:
1. In a 6-qt. Stockpot, heat oil over medium-high heat. Add onions; cook and stir until tender. Add garlic; cook 1 minute longer.
2. Add vinegar, stirring to loosen any browned bits

from pot. Add remaining ingredients; cook 4-6 minutes or until chard is tender, stirring occasionally.

Nutrition Info:
• Per Servings 4g Carbs, 4g Protein, 13g Fat, 144 Calories

Cardamom And Cinnamon Fat Bombs

Servings: 10
Cooking Time: 3 Minutes

Ingredients:
• ¼ tsp ground cardamom (green)
• ¼ tsp ground cinnamon
• ½ cup unsweetened shredded coconut
• ½ tsp vanilla extract
• 3-oz unsalted butter, room temperature

Directions:
1. Place a nonstick pan on medium fire and toast coconut until lightly browned.
2. In a bowl, mix all ingredients.
3. Evenly roll into 10 equal balls.
4. Let it cool in the fridge.
5. Serve and enjoy.

Nutrition Info:
• Per Servings 0.4g Carbs, 0.4g Protein, 10.0g Fat, 90 Calories

Mascarpone Snapped Amaretti Biscuits

Servings: 6
Cooking Time: 25 Minutes

Ingredients:
• 6 egg whites
• 1 egg yolk, beaten
• 1 tsp vanilla bean paste
• 8 oz swerve confectioner's sugar
• A pinch of salt
• ¼ cup ground fragrant almonds
• 1 lemon juice
• 7 tbsp sugar-free amaretto liquor
• ¼ cup mascarpone cheese
• ¼ cup butter, room temperature
• ¾ cup swerve confectioner's sugar, for topping

Directions:
1. Preheat an oven to 300ºF and line a baking sheet with parchment paper. Set aside.
2. In a bowl, beat eggs whites, salt, and vanilla paste with the hand mixer while you gradually spoon in 8 oz of swerve confectioner's sugar until a stiff mixture. Add ground almonds and fold in the egg yolk, lemon

juice, and amaretto liquor. Spoon the mixture into the piping bag and press out 40 to 50 mounds on the baking sheet.
3. Bake the biscuits for 15 minutes by which time they should be golden brown. Whisk the mascarpone cheese, butter, and swerve confectioner's sugar with the cleaned electric mixer; set aside.
4. When the biscuits are ready, transfer them into a serving bowl and let cool. Spread a scoop of mascarpone cream onto one biscuit and snap with another biscuit. Sift some swerve confectioner's sugar on top of them and serve.

Nutrition Info:
• Per Servings 3g Carbs, 9g Protein, 13g Fat, 165 Calories

Parsnip And Carrot Fries With Aioli

Servings: 4
Cooking Time: 40 Minutes

Ingredients:
• 4 tbsp mayonnaise
• 2 garlic cloves, minced
• Salt and black pepper to taste
• 3 tbsp lemon juice
• Parsnip and Carrots Fries:
• 6 medium parsnips, julienned
• 3 large carrots, julienned
• 2 tbsp olive oil
• 5 tbsp chopped parsley
• Salt and black pepper to taste

Directions:
1. Preheat the oven to 400ºF. Make the aioli by mixing the mayonnaise with garlic, salt, pepper, and lemon juice; then refrigerate for 30 minutes.
2. Spread the parsnip and carrots on a baking sheet. Drizzle with olive oil, sprinkle with salt, and pepper, and rub the seasoning into the veggies. Bake for 35 minutes. Remove and transfer to a plate. Garnish the vegetables with parsley and serve with the chilled aioli.

Nutrition Info:
• Per Servings 4.4g Carbs, 2.1g Protein, 4.1g Fat, 205 Calories

Ricotta And Pomegranate

Servings: 3
Cooking Time: 12 Minutes
Ingredients:
- 1 cup Ricotta cheese
- 3 tablespoons olive oil
- 1/2 cup pomegranate Arils
- 2 tsp thyme, fresh
- 2 cups arugula leaves
- Pepper and salt to taste
- 1/2 tsp grated lemon zest

Directions:
1. Mix all ingredients in a bowl.
2. Toss until well combined.
3. Season with pepper and salt.
4. Serve and enjoy.

Nutrition Info:
- Per Servings 9g Carbs, 11g Protein, 25g Fat, 312 Calories

Party Bacon And Pistachio Balls

Servings: 8
Cooking Time: 45 Minutes
Ingredients:
- 8 bacon slices, cooked and chopped
- 8 ounces Liverwurst
- ¼ cup chopped pistachios
- 1 tsp Dijon mustard
- 6 ounces cream cheese

Directions:
1. Combine the liverwurst and pistachios in the bowl of your food processor. Pulse until smooth. Whisk the cream cheese and mustard in another bowl. Make 12 balls out of the liverwurst mixture.
2. Make a thin cream cheese layer over. Coat with bacon, arrange on a plate and chill for 30 minutes.

Nutrition Info:
- Per Servings 1.5g Carbs, 7g Protein, 12g Fat, 145 Calories

Simple Tender Crisp Cauli-bites

Servings: 3
Cooking Time: 10 Minutes
Ingredients:
- 2 cups cauliflower florets
- 2 clove garlic minced
- 4 tablespoons olive oil
- ¼ tsp salt
- ½ tsp pepper

Directions:
1. In a small bowl, mix well olive oil salt, pepper, and garlic.
2. Place cauliflower florets on a baking pan. Drizzle with seasoned oil and toss well to coat.
3. Evenly spread in a single layer and place a pan on the top rack of the oven.
4. Broil on low for 5 minutes. Turnover florets and return to the oven.
5. Continue cooking for another 5 minutes.
6. Serve and enjoy.

Nutrition Info:
- Per Servings 4.9g Carbs, 1.7g Protein, 18g Fat, 183 Calories

Teriyaki Chicken Wings

Servings: 9
Cooking Time: 50 Minutes
Ingredients:
- 3 pounds chicken wings
- 1 onion, chopped
- 2 cups commercial teriyaki sauce
- 1 tablespoon chili garlic paste
- 2 teaspoons ginger paste
- Salt and pepper to taste

Directions:
1. In a heavy-bottomed pot, place on medium-high fire and lightly grease with cooking spray.
2. Pan fry chicken for 4 minutes per side. Cook in two batches.
3. Stir in remaining ingredients in a pot, along with the chicken.
4. Cover and cook on low fire for 30 minutes, stirring every now and then. Continue cooking until desired sauce thickness is achieved.
5. Serve and enjoy.

Nutrition Info:
- Per Servings 5.4g Carbs, 34.3g Protein, 5.4g Fat, 214 Calories

Apricot And Soy Nut Trail Mix

Servings: 20
Cooking Time: 10 Minutes
Ingredients:
- ¼ cup dried apricots, chopped
- 1 cup pumpkin seeds
- ½ cup roasted cashew nuts
- 1 cup roasted, shelled pistachios
- Salt to taste
- 3 tbsp MCT oil or coconut oil

Directions:
1. In a medium mixing bowl, place all ingredients.
2. Thoroughly combine.
3. Bake in the oven for 10 minutes at 3750F.
4. In 20 small zip-top bags, get ¼ cup of the mixture and place in each bag.
5. One zip-top bag is equal to one serving.
6. If properly stored, this can last up to two weeks.

Nutrition Info:
- Per Servings 4.6g Carbs, 5.2g Protein, 10.75g Fat, 129 Calories

Roasted String Beans, Mushrooms & Tomato Plate

Servings: 4
Cooking Time: 32 Minutes
Ingredients:
- 2 cups strings beans, cut in halves
- 1 lb cremini mushrooms, quartered
- 3 tomatoes, quartered
- 2 cloves garlic, minced
- 3 tbsp olive oil
- 3 shallots, julienned
- ½ tsp dried thyme
- Salt and black pepper to season

Directions:
1. Preheat oven to 450ºF. In a bowl, mix the strings beans, mushrooms, tomatoes, garlic, olive oil, shallots, thyme, salt, and pepper. Pour the vegetables in a baking sheet and spread them all around.
2. Place the baking sheet in the oven and bake the veggies for 20 to 25 minutes.

Nutrition Info:
- Per Servings 6g Carbs, 6g Protein, 2g Fat, 121 Calories

Garlicky Cheddar Biscuits

Servings: 4
Cooking Time: 20 Minutes
Ingredients:
- ⅓ cup almond flour
- 2 tsp garlic powder
- Salt to taste
- 1 tsp low carb baking powder
- 5 eggs
- ⅓ cup butter, melted
- 1 ¼ cup grated sharp cheddar cheese
- ⅓ cup Greek yogurt

Directions:
1. Preheat the oven to 350ºF. Mix the flour, garlic powder, salt, baking powder, and cheddar, in a bowl.
2. In a separate bowl, whisk the eggs, butter, and Greek yogurt, and then pour the resulting mixture into the dry ingredients. Stir well until a dough-like consistency has formed.
3. Fetch half soupspoons of the mixture onto a baking sheet with 2-inch intervals between each batter. Bake them in the oven for 12 minutes to be golden brown and remove them after. Serve.

Nutrition Info:
- Per Servings 1.4g Carbs, 5.4g Protein, 14.2g Fat, 153 Calories

Devilled Eggs With Sriracha Mayo

Servings: 4
Cooking Time: 15 Minutes
Ingredients:
- 8 large eggs
- 3 cups water
- Ice water bath
- 3 tbsp sriracha sauce
- 4 tbsp mayonnaise
- Salt to taste
- ¼ tsp smoked paprika

Directions:
1. Bring eggs to boil in salted water in a pot over high heat, and then reduce the heat to simmer for 10 minutes. Transfer eggs to an ice water bath, let cool completely and peel the shells.
2. Slice the eggs in half height wise and empty the yolks into a bowl. Smash with a fork and mix in sriracha sauce, mayonnaise, and half of the paprika until smooth.
3. Spoon filling into a piping bag with a round nozzle

and fill the egg whites to be slightly above the brim. Garnish with remaining paprika and serve immediately.

Nutrition Info:

- Per Servings 1g Carbs, 4g Protein, 19g Fat, 195 Calories

Parmesan Crackers

Servings: 6
Cooking Time: 25 Minutes

Ingredients:

- 1 ⅓ cups coconut flour
- 1 ¼ cup grated Parmesan cheese
- Salt and black pepper to taste
- 1 tsp garlic powder
- ⅓ cup butter, softened
- ⅓ tsp sweet paprika
- ⅓ cup heavy cream
- Water as needed

Directions:

1. Preheat the oven to 350°F.
2. Mix the coconut flour, parmesan cheese, salt, pepper, garlic powder, and paprika in a bowl. Add in the butter and mix well. Top with the heavy cream and mix again until a smooth, thick mixture has formed. Add 1 to 2 tablespoon of water at this point, if it is too thick.
3. Place the dough on a cutting board and cover with plastic wrap. Use a rolling pin to spread out the dough into a light rectangle. Cut cracker squares out of the dough and arrange them on a baking sheet without overlapping. Bake for 20 minutes and transfer to a serving bowl after.

Nutrition Info:

- Per Servings 0.7g Carbs, 5g Protein, 3g Fat, 115 Calories

Buttery Herb Roasted Radishes

Servings: 6
Cooking Time: 25 Minutes

Ingredients:

- 2 lb small radishes, greens removed
- 3 tbsp olive oil
- Salt and black pepper to season
- 3 tbsp unsalted butter
- 1 tbsp chopped parsley
- 1 tbsp chopped tarragon

Directions:

1. Preheat oven to 400°F and line a baking sheet with parchment paper. Toss radishes with oil, salt, and black pepper. Spread on baking sheet and roast for 20 minutes until browned.
2. Heat butter in a large skillet over medium heat to brown and attain a nutty aroma, 2 to 3 minutes.
3. Take out the parsnips from the oven and transfer to a serving plate. Pour over the browned butter atop and sprinkle with parsley and tarragon. Serve with roasted rosemary chicken.

Nutrition Info:

- Per Servings 2g Carbs, 5g Protein, 14g Fat, 160 Calories

Cocoa Nuts Goji Bars

Servings: 6
Cooking Time: 5 Minutes

Ingredients:

- 1 cup raw almonds
- 1 cup raw walnuts
- ¼ tsp cinnamon powder
- ¼ cup dried goji berries
- 1 ½ tsp vanilla extract
- 2 tbsp unsweetened chocolate chips
- 2 tbsp coconut oil
- 1 tbsp golden flax meal
- 1 tsp erythritol

Directions:

1. Combine the walnuts and almonds in the food processor and process at high-speed to be smooth. Add the cinnamon powder, goji berries, vanilla extract, chocolate chips, coconut oil, golden flax meal, and erythritol. Process further until the mixture begins to stick to each other, about 2 minutes.
2. Spread out a large piece of plastic wrap on a flat surface and place the dough on it. Wrap the dough and use a rolling pin to spread it out into a thick rectangle.
3. Unwrap the dough after and use an oiled knife to cut the dough into bars.

Nutrition Info:

- Per Servings 6g Carbs, 2g Protein, 11g Fat, 170 Calories

Italian-style Chicken Wraps

Servings: 8
Cooking Time: 20 Minutes

Ingredients:
- ¼ tsp garlic powder
- 8 ounces provolone cheese
- 8 raw chicken tenders
- Salt and black pepper to taste
- 8 prosciutto slices

Directions:
1. Pound the chicken until half an inch thick. Season with salt, black pepper, and garlic powder. Cut the provolone cheese into 8 strips. Place a slice of prosciutto on a flat surface. Place one chicken tender on top. Top with a provolone strip.
2. Roll the chicken and secure with previously soaked skewers. Grill the wraps for 3 minutes per side.

Nutrition Info:
- Per Servings 0.7g Carbs, 17g Protein, 10g Fat, 174 Calories

Reese Cups

Servings: 12
Cooking Time: 1 Minute

Ingredients:
- ¼ cup unsweetened shredded coconut
- 1 cup almond butter
- ½ cup dark chocolate chips
- 1 tablespoon Stevia
- 1 tablespoon coconut oil

Directions:
1. Line 12 muffin tins with 12 muffin liners.
2. Place the almond butter, honey, and oil in a glass bowl and microwave for 30 seconds or until melted. Divide the mixture into 12 muffin tins. Let it cool for 30 minutes in the fridge.
3. Add the shredded coconuts and mix until evenly distributed.
4. Pour the remaining melted chocolate on top of the coconuts. Freeze for an hour.
5. Carefully remove the chocolates from the muffin tins to create perfect Reese cups.
6. Serve and enjoy.

Nutrition Info:
- Per Servings 10.7g Carbs, 5.0g Protein, 17.1g Fat, 214 Calories

Balsamic Brussels Sprouts With Prosciutto

Servings: 4
Cooking Time: 40 Minutes

Ingredients:
- 3 tbsp balsamic vinegar
- 1 tbsp erythritol
- ½ tbsp olive oil
- Salt and black pepper to taste
- 1 lb Brussels sprouts, halved
- 5 slices prosciutto, chopped

Directions:
1. Preheat oven to 400°F and line a baking sheet with parchment paper. Mix balsamic vinegar, erythritol, olive oil, salt, and black pepper and combine with the brussels sprouts in a bowl.
2. Spread the mixture on the baking sheet and roast for 30 minutes until tender on the inside and crispy on the outside. Toss with prosciutto, share among 4 plates, and serve with chicken breasts.

Nutrition Info:
- Per Servings 0g Carbs, 8g Protein, 14g Fat, 166 Calories

Pork, Beef & Lamb Recipes

Pork, Beef & Lamb Recipes

Beefy Scotch Eggs

Servings: 7
Cooking Time: 25 Minutes

Ingredients:
- 2 eggs, beaten
- 1-pound ground beef
- 2 tablespoons butter, melted
- ¼ cup coconut flour
- 7 large eggs, boiled and peeled
- Cooking spray
- Salt and pepper to taste

Directions:
1. Preheat the oven to 350oF.
2. Place the beaten eggs, ground beef, butter, and coconut flour in a mixing bowl. Season with salt and pepper to taste.
3. Coat the boiled eggs with the meat mixture and place them on a baking sheet.
4. Bake for 25 minutes.

Nutrition Info:
- Per Servings 1.8g Carbs, 21.4g Protein, 25.8g Fat, 312 Calories

Pork Nachos

Servings: 4
Cooking Time: 15 Minutes

Ingredients:
- 1 bag low carb tortilla chips
- 2 cups leftover pulled pork
- 1 red bell pepper, seeded and chopped
- 1 red onion, diced
- 2 cups shredded Monterey Jack cheese

Directions:
1. Preheat oven to 350ºF. Arrange the chips in a medium cast iron pan, scatter pork over, followed by red bell pepper, and onion, and sprinkle with cheese. Place the pan in the oven and cook for 10 minutes until the cheese has melted. Allow cooling for 3 minutes and serve.

Nutrition Info:
- Per Servings 9.3g Carbs, 22g Protein, 25g Fat, 452 Calories

Juicy Pork Medallions

Servings: 4
Cooking Time: 55 Minutes

Ingredients:
- 2 onions, chopped
- 6 bacon slices, chopped
- ½ cup vegetable stock
- Salt and black pepper, to taste
- 1 pound pork tenderloin, cut into medallions

Directions:
1. Set a pan over medium heat, stir in the bacon, cook until crispy, and remove to a plate. Add onions, some pepper, and salt, and cook for 5 minutes; set to the same plate with bacon.
2. Add the pork medallions to the pan, season with pepper and salt, brown for 3 minutes on each side, turn, reduce heat to medium, and cook for 7 minutes. Stir in the stock, and cook for 2 minutes. Return the bacon and onions to the pan and cook for 1 minute.

Nutrition Info:
- Per Servings 6g Carbs, 36g Protein, 18g Fat, 325 Calories

Simple Corned Beef

Servings: 6
Cooking Time: 1 Hour And 30 Minutes

Ingredients:
- 2 pounds corned beef brisket, cut into 1-inch cubes
- 2 cups water
- 2 onions, chopped
- 6 garlic cloves, smashed
- 1 cup olive oil
- 1 tbsp peppercorns
- 1 tsp salt

Directions:
1. Place all ingredients in a heavy-bottomed pot on high fire and bring to a boil.
2. Once boiling, lower fire to a simmer.
3. Simmer for 60 minutes.
4. Turn off fire and shred beef with two forks.
5. Turn on fire and continue cooking until sauce is reduced.
6. Serve and enjoy.

Nutrition Info:
- Per Servings 0.6g Carbs, 12.1g Protein, 30.2g Fat, 314 Calories

Beef Meatballs With Onion Sauce

Servings: 5
Cooking Time: 35 Minutes

Ingredients:
- 2 pounds ground beef
- Salt and black pepper, to taste
- ½ tsp garlic powder
- 1 ¼ tbsp coconut aminos
- 1 cup beef stock
- ¾ cup almond flour
- 1 tbsp fresh parsley, chopped
- 1 tbsp dried onion flakes
- 1 onion, sliced
- 2 tbsp butter
- ¼ cup sour cream

Directions:

1. Using a bowl, combine the beef with salt, garlic powder, almond flour, onion flakes, parsley, 1 tablespoon coconut aminos, black pepper, ¼ cup of beef stock. Form 6 patties, place them on a baking sheet, put in the oven at 370°F, and bake for 18 minutes.

2. Set a pan with the butter over medium heat, stir in the onion, and cook for 3 minutes. Stir in the remaining beef stock, sour cream, and remaining coconut aminos, and bring to a simmer.

3. Remove from heat, adjust the seasoning with black pepper and salt. Serve the meatballs topped with onion sauce.

Nutrition Info:
- Per Servings 6g Carbs, 32g Protein, 23g Fat, 435 Calories

Slow-cooked Beef Moroccan Style

Servings: 8
Cooking Time: 8 Hours

Ingredients:
- ½ cup apricots
- ½ cup sliced yellow onions
- 2 pounds beef roast
- 4 tablespoons garam masala seasoning
- 1 teaspoon sea salt
- 2 cups water

Directions:

1. Place onions and apricots on the bottom of Instant Pot.

2. Rub salt and garam masala all over roast beef and place roast beef on top of onions and apricots.

3. Pour water.

4. Cover, press the slow cook button, adjust cooking time to 6 hours.

5. Once done cooking, remove roast beef and shred with 2 forks.

6. Return to pot, cover, press slow cook, and adjust the time to 2 hours.

7. Serve and enjoy.

Nutrition Info:
- Per Servings 3.0g Carbs, 31.9g Protein, 14.7g Fat, 275 Calories

Beef Cheeseburger Casserole

Servings: 6
Cooking Time: 30 Minutes

Ingredients:
- 2 lb ground beef
- Pink salt and black pepper to taste
- 1 cup cauli rice
- 2 cups chopped cabbage
- 14 oz can diced tomatoes
- ¼ cup water
- 1 cup shredded colby jack cheese

Directions:

1. Preheat oven to 370°F and grease a baking dish with cooking spray. Put beef in a pot and season with salt and black pepper and cook over medium heat for 6 minutes until no longer pink. Drain the grease. Add cauli rice, cabbage, tomatoes, and water. Stir and bring to boil covered for 5 minutes to thicken the sauce. Adjust taste with salt and black pepper.

2. Spoon the beef mixture into the baking dish and spread evenly. Sprinkle with cheese and bake in the oven for 15 minutes until cheese has melted and it's golden brown. Remove and cool for 4 minutes and serve with low carb crusted bread.

Nutrition Info:
- Per Servings 5g Carbs, 20g Protein, 25g Fat, 385 Calories

Jalapeno Beef Pot Roasted

Servings: 4
Cooking Time: 1 Hour 25 Minutes

Ingredients:
- 3½ pounds beef roast
- 4 ounces mushrooms, sliced
- 12 ounces beef stock
- 1 ounce onion soup mix
- ½ cup Italian dressing
- 2 jalapeños, shredded

Directions:
1. Using a bowl, combine the stock with the Italian dressing and onion soup mixture. Place the beef roast in a pan, stir in the stock mixture, mushrooms, and jalapeños; cover with aluminum foil.
2. Set in the oven at 300°F, and bake for 1 hour. Take out the foil and continue baking for 15 minutes. Allow the roast to cool, slice, and serve alongside a topping of the gravy.

Nutrition Info:
- Per Servings 3.2g Carbs, 87g Protein, 46g Fat, 745 Calories

Beef And Ale Pot Roast

Servings: 6
Cooking Time: 2 Hours 20 Minutes

Ingredients:
- 1 ½ lb brisket
- 1 tbsp olive oil
- 8 baby carrots, peeled
- 2 medium red onions, quartered
- 4 stalks celery, cut into chunks
- Salt and black pepper to taste
- 2 bay leaves
- 1 ½ cups low carb beer (ale)

Directions:
1. Preheat the oven to 370°F. Heat the olive oil in a large skillet, while heating, season the brisket with salt and pepper. Brown the meat on both sides for 8 minutes. After, transfer to a deep casserole dish.
2. In the dish, arrange the carrots, onions, celery, and bay leaves around the brisket and pour the beer all over it. Cover the pot and cook the ingredients in the oven for 2 hours.
3. When ready, remove the casserole. Transfer the beef to a chopping board and cut it into thick slices. Serve the beef and vegetables with a drizzle of the sauce and with steamed turnips.

Nutrition Info:
- Per Servings 6g Carbs, 26g Protein, 34g Fat, 513 Calories

Rib Roast With Roasted Red Shallots And Garlic

Servings: 6
Cooking Time: 55 Minutes

Ingredients:
- 5 lb rib roast, on the bone
- 3 heads garlic, cut in half
- 3 tbsp olive oil
- 6 shallots, peeled and halved
- 2 lemons, zested and juiced
- 3 tbsp mustard seeds
- 3 tbsp swerve
- Salt and black pepper to taste
- 3 tbsp thyme leaves

Directions:
1. Preheat the oven to 450°F. Place the garlic heads and shallots in the roasting dish, toss them with olive oil, and cook in the oven for 15 minutes. Pour the lemon juice on them and set aside. Score shallow criss-crosses patterns on the meat and set aside.
2. Mix the swerve, mustard seeds, thyme, salt, pepper, and lemon zest to make a rub; and apply it all over the beef with your hands particularly into the cuts. Place the beef on the shallots and garlic; cook it in the oven for 15 minutes. Reduce the heat to 400°F, cover the top of the dish with foil, and continue cooking for 5 minutes.
3. Once ready, remove the dish, and let the meat sit covered for 15 minutes before slicing. Use the beef pieces in salads or sandwiches.

Nutrition Info:
- Per Servings 2.5g Carbs, 58.4g Protein, 38.6g Fat, 556 Calories

Hot Pork With Dill Pickles

Servings: 4

Cooking Time: 20 Minutes

Ingredients:

- ¼ cup lime juice
- 4 pork chops
- 1 tbsp coconut oil, melted
- 2 garlic cloves, minced
- 1 tbsp chili powder
- 1 tsp ground cinnamon
- 2 tsp cumin
- Salt and black pepper, to taste
- ½ tsp hot pepper sauce
- 4 dill pickles, cut into spears and squeezed

Directions:

1. Using a bowl, combine the lime juice with oil, cumin, salt, hot pepper sauce, pepper, cinnamon, garlic, and chili powder. Place in the pork chops, toss to coat, and refrigerate for 4 hours.

2. Arrange the pork on a preheated grill over medium heat, cook for 7 minutes, turn, add in the dill pickles, and cook for another 7 minutes. Split among serving plates and enjoy.

Nutrition Info:

- Per Servings 2.3g Carbs, 36g Protein, 18g Fat, 315 Calories

Caribbean Beef

Servings: 8

Cooking Time: 1 Hour 10 Minutes

Ingredients:

- 2 onions, chopped
- 2 tbsp avocado oil
- 2 pounds beef stew meat, cubed
- 2 red bell peppers, seeded and chopped
- 1 habanero pepper, chopped
- 4 green chilies, chopped
- 14.5 ounces canned diced tomatoes
- 2 tbsp fresh cilantro, chopped
- 4 garlic cloves, minced
- ½ cup vegetable broth
- Salt and black pepper, to taste
- 1 ½ tsp cumin
- ½ cup black olives, chopped
- 1 tsp dried oregano

Directions:

1. Set a pan over medium-high heat and warm avocado oil. Brown the beef on all sides; remove and set aside. Stir-fry in the red bell peppers, green chilies, oregano, garlic, habanero pepper, onions, and cumin, for about 5-6 minutes. Pour in the tomatoes and broth, and cook for 1 hour. Stir in the olives, adjust the seasonings and serve in bowls sprinkled with fresh cilantro.

Nutrition Info:

- Per Servings 8g Carbs, 25g Protein, 14g Fat, 305 Calories

Smoked Pork Sausages With Mushrooms

Servings: 6

Cooking Time: 1 Hour 10 Minutes

Ingredients:

- 3 yellow bell peppers, seeded and chopped
- 2 pounds smoked sausage, sliced
- Salt and black pepper, to taste
- 2 pounds portobello mushrooms, sliced
- 2 sweet onions, chopped
- 1 tbsp swerve
- 2 tbsp olive oil
- Arugula to garnish

Directions:

1. In a baking dish, combine the sausage slices with swerve, oil, black pepper, onion, bell pepper, salt, and mushrooms. Toss well to ensure everything is coated, set in the oven at 320ºF, and bake for 1 hour. To serve, divide the sausages between plates and scatter over the arugula.

Nutrition Info:

- Per Servings 7.3g Carbs, 29g Protein, 32g Fat, 525 Calories

Ribeye Steak With Shitake Mushrooms

Servings: 1

Cooking Time: 25 Minutes

Ingredients:

- 6 ounces ribeye steak
- 2 tbsp butter
- 1 tsp olive oil
- ½ cup shitake mushrooms, sliced
- Salt and ground pepper, to taste

Directions:

1. Heat the olive oil in a pan over medium heat. Rub the steak with salt and pepper and cook about 4 minutes per side; set aside. Melt the butter in the pan and cook the shitakes for 4 minutes. Pour the butter and mushrooms over the steak to serve.

Nutrition Info:
• Per Servings 3g Carbs, 33g Protein, 31g Fat, 478 Calories

Pork Lettuce Cups

Servings: 6
Cooking Time: 20 Minutes

Ingredients:
• 2 lb ground pork
• 1 tbsp ginger- garlic paste
• Pink salt and chili pepper to taste
• 1 tsp ghee
• 1 head Iceberg lettuce
• 2 sprigs green onion, chopped
• 1 red bell pepper, seeded and chopped
• ½ cucumber, finely chopped

Directions:
1. Put the pork with ginger-garlic paste, salt, and chili pepper seasoning in a saucepan. Cook for 10 minutes over medium heat while breaking any lumps until the pork is no longer pink. Drain liquid and add the ghee, melt and brown the meat for 4 minutes, continuously stirring. Turn the heat off.
2. Pat the lettuce dry with paper towel and in each leaf, spoon two to three tablespoons of pork, top with green onions, bell pepper, and cucumber. Serve with soy drizzling sauce.

Nutrition Info:
• Per Servings 1g Carbs, 19g Protein, 24.3g Fat, 311 Calories

Spicy Pork Stew With Spinach

Servings: 4
Cooking Time: 40 Minutes

Ingredients:
• 1 lb. pork butt, cut into chunks
• 1 onion, chopped
• 4 cloves of garlic, minced
• 1 cup coconut milk, freshly squeezed
• 1 cup spinach leaves, washed and rinsed
• Salt and pepper to taste
• 1 cup water

Directions:
1. In a heavy-bottomed pot, add all ingredients, except for coconut milk and spinach. Mix well.
2. Cover and cook on medium-high fire until boiling. Lower fire to a simmer and cook for 30 minutes undisturbed.
3. Add remaining ingredients and cook on high fire

uncovered for 5 minutes. Adjust seasoning if needed.
4. Serve and enjoy.

Nutrition Info:
• Per Servings 7.2g Carbs, 30.5g Protein, 34.4g Fat, 458 Calories

Beef Sausage Casserole

Servings: 8
Cooking Time: 60 Minutes

Ingredients:
• ⅓ cup almond flour
• 2 eggs
• 2 pounds beef sausage, chopped
• Salt and black pepper, to taste
• 1 tbsp dried parsley
• ¼ tsp red pepper flakes
• ¼ cup Parmesan cheese, grated
• ¼ tsp onion powder
• ½ tsp garlic powder
• ¼ tsp dried oregano
• 1 cup ricotta cheese
• 1 cup sugar-free marinara sauce
• 1½ cups cheddar cheese, shredded

Directions:
1. Using a bowl, combine the sausage, pepper, pepper flakes, oregano, eggs, Parmesan cheese, onion powder, almond flour, salt, parsley, and garlic powder. Form balls, lay them on a lined baking sheet, place in the oven at 370ºF, and bake for 15 minutes.
2. Remove the balls from the oven and cover with half of the marinara sauce. Pour ricotta cheese all over followed by the rest of the marinara sauce. Scatter the cheddar cheese and bake in the oven for 10 minutes. Allow the meatballs casserole to cool before serving.

Nutrition Info:
• Per Servings 4g Carbs, 32g Protein, 35g Fat, 456 Calories

Keto Beefy Burritos

Servings: 6
Cooking Time: 25 Minutes

Ingredients:
• 1-pound lean ground beef
• 6 large kale leaves
• 1/4 cup onion
• 1/4 cup low-sodium tomato puree
• 1/4 teaspoon ground cumin
• What you'll need from the store cupboard:
• 1/4 teaspoon black pepper

- ½ tsp salt

Directions:

1. In a medium skillet, brown ground beef for 15 minutes; drain oil on paper towels.
2. Spray skillet with non-stick cooking spray; add onion to cook for 3-5 minutes, until vegetables are softened.
3. Add beef, tomato puree, black pepper, and cumin to onion/pepper mixture.
4. Mix well and cook for 3 to 5 minutes on low heat.
5. Divide the beef mixture among kale leaves.
6. Roll the kale leaves over burrito style, making sure that both ends are folded first, so the mixture does not fall out. Secure with a toothpick.

Nutrition Info:

- Per Servings 6.0g Carbs, 25.0g Protein, 32.0g Fat, 412 Calories

Lettuce Taco Carnitas

Servings: 12
Cooking Time: 40 Minutes

Ingredients:

- 2 cups shredded Colby-Monterey jack cheese
- 1 can green chilies and diced tomatoes, undrained
- 1 envelope taco seasoning
- 1 boneless pork shoulder butt roast
- Lettuce leaves
- Pepper and salt to taste
- 1 cup water

Directions:

1. Add all ingredients in a pot, except for cheese and lettuce leaves, on high fire, and bring to a boil.
2. Once boiling, lower fire to a simmer and cook for 35 minutes.
3. Adjust seasoning to taste.
4. To serve, add a good amount of shredded pork into the center of one lettuce leaf. Top it with cheese, roll, and enjoy.

Nutrition Info:

- Per Servings 1.7g Carbs, 28.5g Protein, 10.4g Fat, 214 Calories

Garlic Pork Chops With Mint Pesto

Servings: 4
Cooking Time: 3 Hours 10 Minutes

Ingredients:

- 1 cup parsley
- 1 cup mint

- 1½ onions, chopped
- ⅓ cup pistachios
- 1 tsp lemon zest
- 5 tbsp avocado oil
- Salt, to taste
- 4 pork chops
- 5 garlic cloves, minced
- Juice from 1 lemon

Directions:

1. In a food processor, combine the parsley with avocado oil, mint, pistachios, salt, lemon zest, and 1 onion. Rub the pork with this mixture, place in a bowl, and refrigerate for 1 hour while covered.
2. Remove the chops and set to a baking dish, place in ½ onion, and garlic; sprinkle with lemon juice, and bake for 2 hours in the oven at 250ºF. Split amongst plates and enjoy.

Nutrition Info:

- Per Servings 5.5g Carbs, 37g Protein, 40g Fat, 567 Calories

Dr. Pepper Pulled Pork

Servings: 9
Cooking Time: 45 Minutes

Ingredients:

- 3 pounds pork loin roast, chopped into 8 equal pieces
- 1 packet pork rub seasoning
- 1 12-ounce can Dr. Pepper
- ½ cup commercial BBQ sauce
- 1 bay leaf
- 1 tsp oil
- 2 tbsp water

Directions:

1. Place a heavy-bottomed pot on medium-high fire and heat for 2 minutes. Add oil and swirl to coat the bottom and sides of pot and heat for a minute.
2. Brown roast for 4 minutes per side.
3. Add remaining ingredients.
4. Cover and simmer for 30 minutes or until pork is fork-tender. Stir the bottom of the pot every now and then. Turn off the fire.
5. With two forks, shred pork.
6. Turn on fire to high and boil uncovered until sauce is rendered, around 5 minutes.
7. Serve and enjoy.

Nutrition Info:

- Per Servings 4.6g Carbs, 40.9g Protein, 13.4g Fat, 310 Calories

Peanut Butter Pork Stir-fry

Servings: 4
Cooking Time: 23 Minutes

Ingredients:
- 1 ½ tbsp ghee
- 2 lb pork loin, cut into strips
- Pink salt and chili pepper to taste
- 2 tsp ginger- garlic paste
- ¼ cup chicken broth
- 5 tbsp peanut butter
- 2 cups mixed stir-fry vegetables

Directions:
1. Melt the ghee in a wok and mix the pork with salt, chili pepper, and ginger-garlic paste. Pour the pork into the wok and cook for 6 minutes until no longer pink.
2. Mix the peanut butter with some broth to be smooth, add to the pork and stir; cook for 2 minutes. Pour in the remaining broth, cook for 4 minutes, and add the mixed veggies. Simmer for 5 minutes.
3. Adjust the taste with salt and black pepper, and spoon the stir-fry to a side of cilantro cauli rice.

Nutrition Info:
- Per Servings 1g Carbs, 22.5g Protein, 49g Fat, 571 Calories

Balsamic Grilled Pork Chops

Servings: 6
Cooking Time: 2 Hours 20 Minutes

Ingredients:
- 6 pork loin chops, boneless
- 2 tbsp erythritol
- ¼ cup balsamic vinegar
- 3 cloves garlic, minced
- ¼ cup olive oil
- ⅓ tsp salt
- Black pepper to taste

Directions:
1. Put the pork in a plastic bag. In a bowl, mix the erythritol, balsamic vinegar, garlic, olive oil, salt, pepper, and pour the sauce over the pork. Seal the bag, shake it, and place in the refrigerator.
2. Marinate the pork for 1 to 2 hours. Preheat the grill on medium-high heat, remove the pork when ready, and grill covered for 10 to 12 minutes on each side. Remove the pork chops, let them sit for 4 minutes, and serve with a syrupy parsnip sauté.

Nutrition Info:
- Per Servings 1.5g Carbs, 38.1g Protein, 26.8g Fat, 418 Calories

Pork Goulash With Cauliflower

Servings: 4
Cooking Time: 15 Minutes

Ingredients:
- 1 red bell pepper, seeded and chopped
- 2 tbsp olive oil
- 1½ pounds ground pork
- Salt and black pepper, to taste
- 2 cups cauliflower florets
- 1 onion, chopped
- 14 ounces canned diced tomatoes
- ¼ tsp garlic powder
- 1 tbsp tomato puree
- 1 ½ cups water

Directions:
1. Heat olive oil in a pan over medium heat, stir in the pork, and brown for 5 minutes. Place in the bell pepper and onion, and cook for 4 minutes. Stir in the water, tomatoes, and cauliflower, bring to a simmer and cook for 5 minutes while covered. Place in the pepper, tomato paste, salt, and garlic powder. Stir well, remove from the heat, split into bowls, and enjoy with keto bread.

Nutrition Info:
- Per Servings 4.5g Carbs, 44g Protein, 37g Fat, 475 Calories

Beef Stovies

Servings: 4
Cooking Time: 60 Minutes

Ingredients:
- 1 lb ground beef
- 1 large onion, chopped
- 6 parsnips, peeled and chopped
- 1 large carrot, chopped
- 1 tbsp olive oil
- 1 clove garlic, minced
- Salt and black pepper to taste
- 1 cup chicken broth
- ¼ tsp allspice
- 2 tsp rosemary leaves
- 1 tbsp sugar-free Worcestershire sauce
- ½ small cabbage, shredded

Directions:
1. Heat the oil in a skillet over medium heat and cook the beef for 4 minutes. Season with salt and pepper, and occasionally stir while breaking the lumps in it.

2. Add the onion, garlic, carrots, rosemary, and parsnips. Stir and cook for a minute, and pour the chicken broth, allspice, and Worcestershire sauce in it. Stir the mixture and cook the ingredients on low heat for 40 minutes.

3. Stir in the cabbage, season with salt and pepper, and cook the ingredients further for 2 minutes. After, turn the heat off, plate the stovies, and serve with wilted spinach and collards.

Nutrition Info:
- Per Servings 3g Carbs, 14g Protein, 18g Fat, 316 Calories

Mustardy Pork Chops

Servings: 4
Cooking Time: 15 Minutes

Ingredients:
- 4 pork loin chops
- 1 tsp Dijon mustard
- 1 tbsp soy sauce
- 1 tsp lemon juice
- 1 tbsp water
- Salt and black pepper, to taste
- 1 tbsp butter
- A bunch of scallions, chopped

Directions:
1. Using a bowl, combine the water with lemon juice, mustard and soy sauce. Set a pan over medium heat and warm butter, add in the pork chops, season with salt, and pepper, cook for 4 minutes, turn, and cook for additional 4 minutes. Remove the pork chops to a plate and keep warm.

2. In the same pan, pour in the mustard sauce, and simmer for 5 minutes. Spread this over pork, top with scallions, and enjoy.

Nutrition Info:
- Per Servings 1.2g Carbs, 38g Protein, 21.5g Fat, 382 Calories

Baked Pork Meatballs In Pasta Sauce

Servings: 6
Cooking Time: 45 Minutes

Ingredients:
- 2 lb ground pork
- 1 tbsp olive oil
- 1 cup pork rinds, crushed
- 3 cloves garlic, minced
- ½ cup coconut milk
- 2 eggs, beaten
- ½ cup grated Parmesan cheese
- ½ cup grated asiago cheese
- Salt and black pepper to taste
- ¼ cup chopped parsley
- 2 jars sugar-free marinara sauce
- ½ tsp Italian seasoning
- 1 cup Italian blend kinds of cheeses
- Chopped basil to garnish
- Cooking spray

Directions:
1. Preheat the oven to 400ºF, line a cast iron pan with foil and oil it with cooking spray. Set aside.

2. Combine the coconut milk and pork rinds in a bowl. Mix in the ground pork, garlic, Asiago cheese, Parmesan cheese, eggs, salt, and pepper, just until combined. Form balls of the mixture and place them in the prepared pan. Bake in the oven for 20 minutes at a reduced temperature of 370ºF.

3. Transfer the meatballs to a plate. Remove the foil and pour in half of the marinara sauce. Place the meatballs back in the pan and pour the remaining marinara sauce all over them. Sprinkle all over with the Italian blend cheeses, drizzle the olive oil on them, and then sprinkle with Italian seasoning.

4. Cover the pan with foil and put it back in the oven to bake for 10 minutes. After, remove the foil, and continue cooking for 5 minutes. Once ready, take out the pan and garnish with basil. Serve on a bed of squash spaghetti.

Nutrition Info:
- Per Servings 4.1g Carbs, 46.2g Protein, 46.8g Fat, 590 Calories

Garlic Crispy Pork Loin

Servings: 4
Cooking Time: 1h 5 Minutes

Ingredients:
- 1 quart cold water
- 3 cloves garlic, crushed
- 3 tablespoons. chopped fresh ginger
- 1 boneless pork loin roast
- 2 tablespoons. Dijon mustard
- Salt and freshly ground black pepper to taste
- 2 teaspoons. dried rosemary
- 1 tablespoon olive oil
- 2 tablespoons stevia
- 1/2 teaspoon red pepper flakes

Directions:
1. Mix water, salt, 1 tbsp. stevia, garlic, ginger, rose-

mary and red pepper flakes in a large bowl.

2. Place pork loin in brine mixture and refrigerate for 8 to 10 hours. Remove pork from brine, pat dry, and season all sides with salt and black pepper.

3. Preheat oven to 325 degrees F.

4. Heat olive oil in a skillet over high heat. Cook pork for about 10 minutes.

5. Transfer skillet to the oven and roast for about 40 minutes.

6. Mix 2 tablespoons stevia and Dijon mustard together in a small bowl.

7. Remove pork roast from the oven and spread stevia mixture on all sides. Cook for an additional 15 minutes at 145 degrees F. Serve and enjoy.

Nutrition Info:

• Per Servings 19.3g Carbs, 30.7g Protein, 18.9g Fat, 376 Calories

Cocoa-crusted Pork Tenderloin

Servings: 2
Cooking Time: 25 Minutes

Ingredients:

• 1-pound pork tenderloin, trimmed from fat
• 1 tablespoon cocoa powder
• 1 teaspoon instant coffee powder
• ½ teaspoon ground cinnamon
• ½ teaspoon chili powder
• 1 tablespoon olive oil
• Pepper and salt to taste

Directions:

1. In a bowl, dust the pork tenderloin with cocoa powder, coffee, cinnamon, pepper, salt, and chili powder.

2. In a skillet, heat the oil and sear the meat for 5 minutes on both sides over low to medium flame.

3. Transfer the pork in a baking dish and cook in the oven for 15 minutes in a 350F preheated oven.

Nutrition Info:

• Per Servings 2.0g Carbs, 60.0g Protein, 15.0g Fat, 395 Calories

Seasoned Garlic Pork Chops

Servings: 8
Cooking Time: 10 Mins

Ingredients:

• 1/2 cup water
• 1/3 cup mayo
• 3 tablespoons lemon pepper seasoning
• 2 teaspoons minced garlic
• 6 boneless pork loin chops, trimmed of fat

• 1/4 cup olive oil

Directions:

1. Mix water, mayo, olive oil, lemon pepper seasoning, and minced garlic in a deep bowl.

2. Add pork chops and marinate in refrigerator at least 2 hours.

3. Preheat an outdoor grill at medium-high heat and lightly oil the grate.

4. Remove pork chops and cook on the preheated grill for 5 to 6 minutes per side at 145 degrees F.

5. Serve and enjoy.

Nutrition Info:

• Per Servings 2.1g Carbs, 40.7g Protein, 22g Fat, 380 Calories

Italian Sausage Stew

Servings: 6
Cooking Time: 35 Minutes

Ingredients:

• 1 pound Italian sausage, sliced
• 1 red bell pepper, seeded and chopped
• 2 onions, chopped
• Salt and black pepper, to taste
• 1 cup fresh parsley, chopped
• 6 green onions, chopped
• ¼ cup avocado oil
• 1 cup beef stock
• 4 garlic cloves
• 24 ounces canned diced tomatoes
• 16 ounces okra, trimmed and sliced
• 6 ounces tomato sauce
• 2 tbsp coconut aminos
• 1 tbsp hot sauce

Directions:

1. Set a pot over medium-high heat and warm oil, place in the sausages, and cook for 2 minutes. Stir in the onion, green onions, garlic, pepper, bell pepper, and salt, and cook for 5 minutes.

2. Add in the hot sauce, stock, tomatoes, coconut aminos, okra, and tomato sauce, bring to a simmer and cook for 15 minutes. Adjust the seasoning with salt and pepper. Share into serving bowls and sprinkle with fresh parsley to serve.

Nutrition Info:

• Per Servings 7g Carbs, 16g Protein, 25g Fat, 314 Calories

Bistro Beef Tenderloin

Servings: 7
Cooking Time: 45 Minutes

Ingredients:
- 1 3-pound beef tenderloin, trimmed of fat
- 2/3 cup chopped mixed herbs
- 2 tablespoons Dijon mustard
- 5 tablespoons extra virgin olive oil
- ½ teaspoon ground black pepper
- ½ tsp salt

Directions:
1. Preheat the oven to 400F.
2. Secure the beef tenderloin with a string in three places so that it does not flatten while roasting.
3. Place the beef tenderloin in a dish and rub onto the meat the olive oil, black pepper, salt, and mixed herb.
4. Place on a roasting pan and cook in the oven for 45 minutes.
5. Roast until the thermometer inserted into the thickest part of the meat until it registers 1400F for medium rare.
6. Place the tenderloin on a chopping board and remove the string. Slice into 1-inch thick slices and brush with Dijon mustard.

Nutrition Info:
- Per Servings 0.6g Carbs, 59.0g Protein, 22.0g Fat, 440 Calories

Zucchini Boats With Beef And Pimiento Rojo

Servings: 4
Cooking Time: 30 Minutes

Ingredients:
- 4 zucchinis
- 2 tbsp olive oil
- 1 ½ lb ground beef
- 1 medium red onion, chopped
- 2 tbsp chopped pimiento
- Pink salt and black pepper to taste
- 1 cup grated yellow cheddar cheese

Directions:
1. Preheat oven to 350ºF.
2. Lay the zucchinis on a flat surface, trim off the ends and cut in half lengthwise. Scoop out pulp from each half with a spoon to make shells. Chop the pulp.
3. Heat oil in a skillet; add the ground beef, red onion, pimiento, and zucchini pulp, and season with salt and black pepper. Cook for 6 minutes while stirring

to break up lumps until beef is no longer pink. Turn the heat off. Spoon the beef into the boats and sprinkle with cheddar cheese.
4. Place on a greased baking sheet and cook to melt the cheese for 15 minutes until zucchini boats are tender. Take out, cool for 2 minutes, and serve warm with a mixed green salad.

Nutrition Info:
- Per Servings 7g Carbs, 18g Protein, 24g Fat, 335 Calories

Italian Beef Ragout

Servings: 4
Cooking Time: 1 Hour 52 Minutes

Ingredients:
- 1 lb chuck steak, trimmed and cubed
- 2 tbsp olive oil
- Salt and black pepper to taste
- 2 tbsp almond flour
- 1 medium onion, diced
- ½ cup dry white wine
- 1 red bell pepper, seeded and diced
- 2 tsp sugar-free Worcestershire sauce
- 4 oz tomato puree
- 3 tsp smoked paprika
- 1 cup beef broth
- Thyme leaves to garnish

Directions:
1. First, lightly dredge the meat in the almond flour and set aside. Place a large skillet over medium heat, add 1 tablespoon of oil to heat and then sauté the onion, and bell pepper for 3 minutes. Stir in the paprika, and add the remaining olive oil.
2. Add the beef and cook for 10 minutes in total while turning them halfway. Stir in white wine, let it reduce by half, about 3 minutes, and add Worcestershire sauce, tomato puree, and beef broth.
3. Let the mixture boil for 2 minutes, then reduce the heat to lowest and let simmer for 1 ½ hours; stirring now and then. Adjust the taste and dish the ragout. Serve garnished with thyme leaves.

Nutrition Info:
- Per Servings 4.2g Carbs, 36.6g Protein, 21.6g Fat, 328 Calories

Spicy Spinach Pinwheel Steaks

Servings: 6
Cooking Time: 42 Minutes

Ingredients:
- Cooking spray
- 1 ½ lb flank steak
- Pink salt and black pepper to season
- 1 cup crumbled feta cheese
- ½ loose cup baby spinach
- 1 jalapeño, chopped
- ¼ cup chopped basil leaves

Directions:
1. Preheat oven to 400ºF and grease a baking sheet with cooking spray.
2. Wrap the steak in plastic wrap, place on a flat surface, and gently run a rolling pin over to flatten. Take off the wraps. Sprinkle with half of the feta cheese, top with spinach, jalapeno, basil leaves, and the remaining cheese. Roll the steak over on the stuffing and secure with toothpicks.
3. Place in the greased baking sheet and cook for 30 minutes, flipping once until nicely browned on the outside and the cheese melted within. Cool for 3 minutes, slice into pinwheels and serve with thyme sautéed mixed veggies.

Nutrition Info:
- Per Servings 2g Carbs, 28g Protein, 41g Fat, 490 Calories

Easy Thai 5-spice Pork Stew

Servings: 9
Cooking Time: 40 Minutes

Ingredients:
- 2 lb. pork butt, cut into chunks
- 2 tbsp. 5-spice powder
- 2 cups coconut milk, freshly squeezed
- 1 ½ tbsp sliced ginger
- 1 cup chopped cilantro
- 1 tsp oil
- Salt and pepper to taste
- ½ cup water

Directions:
1. Place a heavy-bottomed pot on medium-high fire and heat for 2 minutes. Add oil and heat for a minute.
2. Stir in pork chunks and cook for 3 minutes per side.
3. Add ginger, cilantro, pepper, and salt. Sauté for 2 minutes.
4. Add water and deglaze the pot. Stir in 5-spice powder.
5. Cover and simmer for 20 minutes.
6. Stir in coconut milk. Cover and cook for another 10 minutes.
7. Adjust seasoning if needed.
8. Serve and enjoy.

Nutrition Info:
- Per Servings 4.4g Carbs, 39.8g Protein, 30.5g Fat, 398 Calories

Pork Osso Bucco

Servings: 6
Cooking Time: 1 Hour 55 Minutes

Ingredients:
- 4 tbsp butter, softened
- 6 pork shanks
- 2 tbsp olive oil
- 3 cloves garlic, minced
- 1 cup diced tomatoes
- Salt and black pepper to taste
- ½ cup chopped onions
- ½ cup chopped celery
- ½ cup chopped carrots
- 2 cups Cabernet Sauvignon
- 5 cups beef broth
- ½ cup chopped parsley + extra to garnish
- 2 tsp lemon zest

Directions:
1. Melt the butter in a large saucepan over medium heat. Season the pork with salt and pepper and brown it for 12 minutes; remove to a plate.
2. In the same pan, sauté 2 cloves of garlic and onions in the oil, for 3 minutes then return the pork shanks. Stir in the Cabernet, carrots, celery, tomatoes, and beef broth with a season of salt and pepper. Cover the pan and let it simmer on low heat for 1 ½ hours basting the pork every 15 minutes with the sauce.
3. In a bowl, mix the remaining garlic, parsley, and lemon zest to make a gremolata, and stir the mixture into the sauce when it is ready. Turn the heat off and dish the Osso Bucco. Garnish with parsley and serve with a creamy turnip mash.

Nutrition Info:
- Per Servings 6.1g Carbs, 34g Protein, 40g Fat, 590 Calories

New York Strip Steak With Mushroom Sauce

Servings: 2
Cooking Time: 20 Minutes

Ingredients:

- 2 New York Strip steaks, trimmed from fat
- 3 cloves of garlic, minced
- 2 ounces shiitake mushrooms, sliced
- 2 ounces button mushrooms, sliced
- ¼ teaspoon thyme
- ¼ cup water
- ½ tsp salt
- 1 tsp pepper
- 5 tablespoons olive oil

Directions:

1. Heat the grill to 350F.
2. Position the grill rack 6 inches from the heat source.
3. Grill the steak for 10 minutes on each side or until slightly pink on the inside.
4. Meanwhile, prepare the sauce. In a small nonstick pan, water sauté the garlic, mushrooms, salt, pepper, and thyme for a minute. Pour in the broth and bring to a boil. Allow the sauce to simmer until the liquid is reduced.
5. Top the steaks with the mushroom sauce. Drizzle with olive oil.
6. Serve warm.

Nutrition Info:

- Per Servings 4.0g Carbs, 47.0g Protein, 36.0g Fat, 528 Calories

Pecorino Veal Cutlets

Servings: 6
Cooking Time: 1 Hour 15 Minutes

Ingredients:

- 6 veal cutlets
- ½ cup Pecorino cheese, grated
- 6 Provolone cheese slices
- Salt and black pepper, to taste
- 4 cups tomato sauce
- A pinch of garlic salt
- Cooking spray
- 2 tbsp butter
- 2 tbsp coconut oil, melted
- 1 tsp Italian seasoning

Directions:

1. Season the veal cutlets with garlic salt, pepper, and salt. Set a pan over medium-high heat and warm oil and butter, place in the veal, and cook until browned on all sides. Spread half of the tomato sauce on the bottom of a baking dish that is coated with some cooking spray.
2. Place in the veal cutlets then spread with Italian seasoning and sprinkle over the remaining sauce. Set in the oven at 360° F, and bake for 40 minutes.
3. Spread with the Provolone cheese, then sprinkle with the Pecorino cheese, and bake in the oven for 5 minutes until the cheese is golden and melted. Serve immediately.

Nutrition Info:

- Per Servings 6g Carbs, 26g Protein, 21g Fat, 362 Calories

Poultry Recipes

Poultry Recipes

Chicken Drumsticks In Tomato Sauce

Servings: 4

Cooking Time: 1 Hour 35 Minutes

Ingredients:

- 8 chicken drumsticks
- 1 ½ tbsp olive oil
- 1 medium white onion, diced
- 3 medium turnips, peeled and diced
- 2 medium carrots, chopped in 1-inch pieces
- 2 green bell peppers, seeded, cut into chunks
- 2 cloves garlic, minced
- ¼ cup coconut flour
- 1 cup chicken broth
- 1 can sugar-free tomato sauce
- 2 tbsp dried Italian herbs
- Salt and black pepper to taste

Directions:

1. Preheat oven to 400ºF.
2. Heat the oil in a large skillet over medium heat, meanwhile season the drumsticks with salt and pepper, and fry them in the oil to brown on both sides for 10 minutes. Remove to a baking dish.
3. Next, sauté the onion, turnips, bell peppers, carrots, and garlic in the same oil and for 10 minutes with continuous stirring.
4. Then, in a bowl, evenly combine the broth, coconut flour, tomato paste, and Italian herbs together, and pour it over the vegetables in the pan. Stir and cook to thicken for 4 minutes.
5. Turn the heat off and pour the mixture on the chicken in the baking dish. Bake the chicken and vegetables in the oven for around 1 hour. Remove from the oven and serve with steamed cauli rice.

Nutrition Info:

- Per Servings 7.3g Carbs, 50.8g Protein, 34.2g Fat, 515 Calories

Simple Chicken Garlic-tomato Stew

Servings: 4

Cooking Time: 45 Minutes

Ingredients:

- 3 tbsp. coconut oil
- 5 cloves of garlic, minced
- 4 chicken breasts halves
- 3 roma tomatoes chopped
- 1 small onion chopped
- Salt and pepper to taste
- 1 ½ cups water

Directions:

1. Place a large saucepan on medium-high fire and heat for 2 minutes.
2. Add 1 tbsp oil and heat for a minute.
3. Season chicken breasts generously with pepper and salt.
4. Sear for 5 minutes per side of the chicken breast. Transfer to a plate and let it rest.
5. In the same pan, add remaining oil and sauté garlic for a minute. Stir in onions and tomatoes. Sauté for 7 minutes.
6. Meanwhile, chop chicken into bite-sized pieces.
7. Deglaze pan with water and add chopped chicken. Cover and simmer for 15 minutes.
8. Adjust seasoning if needed.
9. Serve and enjoy.

Nutrition Info:

- Per Servings 1.1g Carbs, 60.8g Protein, 37.5g Fat, 591 Calories

Chicken Thighs With Broccoli & Green Onions

Servings: 2
Cooking Time: 25 Minutes

Ingredients:
- 2 chicken thighs, skinless, boneless, cut into strips
- 1 tbsp olive oil
- 1 tsp red pepper flakes
- 1 tsp onion powder
- 1 tbsp fresh ginger, grated
- ¼ cup tamari sauce
- ½ tsp garlic powder
- ½ cup water
- ½ cup erythritol
- ½ tsp xanthan gum
- ½ cup green onions, chopped
- 1 small head broccoli, cut into florets

Directions:
1. Set a pan over medium heat and warm oil, cook in the chicken and ginger for 4 minutes. Stir in the water, onion powder, pepper flakes, garlic powder, tamari sauce, xanthan gum, and erythritol, and cook for 15 minutes. Add in the green onions and broccoli, cook for 6 minutes. Serve hot.

Nutrition Info:
- Per Servings 5g Carbs, 27g Protein, 23g Fat, 387 Calories

Turkey & Mushroom Bake

Servings: 8
Cooking Time: 55 Minutes

Ingredients:
- 4 cups mushrooms, sliced
- 1 egg, whisked
- 3 cups green cabbage, shredded
- 3 cups turkey meat, cooked and chopped
- ½ cup chicken stock
- ½ cup cream cheese
- 1 tsp poultry seasoning
- 2 cup cheddar cheese, grated
- ½ cup Parmesan cheese, grated
- Salt and ground black pepper, to taste
- ¼ tsp garlic powder

Directions:
1. Set a pan over medium-low heat. Stir in chicken broth, egg, Parmesan cheese, pepper, garlic powder, poultry seasoning, cheddar cheese, cream cheese, and salt, and simmer.

2. Place in the cabbage and turkey meat, and set away from the heat.
3. Add the mushrooms, pepper, turkey mixture and salt in a baking dish and spread. Place aluminum foil to cover, set in an oven at 390ºF, and bake for 35 minutes. Allow cooling and enjoy.

Nutrition Info:
- Per Servings 3g Carbs, 25g Protein, 15g Fat, 245 Calories

Bacon & Cheese Chicken

Servings: 4
Cooking Time: 30 Minutes

Ingredients:
- 4 bacon strips
- 4 chicken breasts
- 3 green onions, chopped
- 4 ounces ranch dressing
- 1 ounce coconut aminos
- 2 tbsp coconut oil
- 4 oz Monterey Jack cheese, grated

Directions:
1. Set a pan over high heat and warm the oil. Place in the chicken breasts, cook for 7 minutes, then flip to the other side; cook for an additional 7 minutes. Set another pan over medium-high heat, place in the bacon, cook until crispy, remove to paper towels, drain the grease, and crumble.

2. Add the chicken breast to a baking dish. Place the green onions, coconut aminos, cheese, and crumbled bacon on top, set in an oven, turn on the broiler, and cook for 5 minutes at high temperature. Split among serving plates and serve.

Nutrition Info:
- Per Servings 3.3g Carbs, 34g Protein, 21g Fat, 423 Calories

Heart Healthy Chicken Salad

Servings: 4
Cooking Time: 45 Minutes

Ingredients:
- 3 tbsp mayonnaise, low-fat
- ½ tsp onion powder
- 1 tbsp lemon juice
- ¼ cup celery (chopped)
- 3 ¼ cups chicken breast (cooked, cubed, and skinless)
- Salt and pepper to taste

Directions:
1. Bake chicken breasts for 45 minutes at 350oF. Let it cool and cut them into cubes and place them in the refrigerator.
2. Combine all other ingredients in a large bowl then add the chilled chicken.
3. Mix well and ready to serve.
4. Enjoy!

Nutrition Info:
- Per Servings 1.0g Carbs, 50.0g Protein, 22.0g Fat, 408 Calories

Chicken Country Style

Servings: 4
Cooking Time: 25 Minutes

Ingredients:
- 3 tablespoons butter
- 1 packet dry Lipton's onion soup mix
- 1 can Campbell's chicken gravy
- 4 skinless and boneless chicken breasts
- 1/3 teaspoon pepper
- 1 cup water

Directions:
1. Add all ingredients in a pot on high fire and bring it to a boil.
2. Once boiling, lower fire to a simmer and cook for 25 minutes.
3. Adjust seasoning to taste.
4. Serve and enjoy.

Nutrition Info:
- Per Servings 6.8g Carbs, 53.7g Protein, 16.9g Fat, 380 Calories

Whole Roasted Chicken With Lemon And Rosemary

Servings: 12
Cooking Time: 1 Hour And 40 Minutes

Ingredients:
- 1 whole chicken
- 6 cloves of garlic, minced
- 1 lemon, sliced
- 2 sprigs rosemary
- Salt and pepper to taste

Directions:
1. Place lemon peel, 1 rosemary sprig, and 2 cloves of smashed garlic in chicken cavity.
2. Place the whole chicken in a big bowl and rub all the spices onto the surface and insides of the chicken.
3. Place the chicken on a wire rack placed on top of a baking pan. Tent with foil.
4. Cook in a preheated 350oF oven for 60 minutes.
5. Remove foil and continue baking until golden brown, around 30 minutes more.
6. Let chicken rest for 10 minutes.
7. Serve and enjoy.

Nutrition Info:
- Per Servings 0.9g Carbs, 21.3g Protein, 17.2g Fat, 248 Calories

Lemon & Rosemary Chicken In A Skillet

Servings: 4
Cooking Time: 1 Hour And 20 Minutes

Ingredients:
- 8 chicken thighs
- 1 tsp salt
- 2 tbsp lemon juice
- 1 tsp lemon zest
- 2 tbsp olive oil
- 1 tbsp chopped rosemary
- ¼ tsp black pepper
- 1 garlic clove, minced

Directions:
1. Combine all ingredients in a bowl. Place in the fridge for one hour.
2. Heat a skillet over medium heat. Add the chicken along with the juices and cook until crispy, about 7 minutes per side.

Nutrition Info:
- Per Servings 2.5g Carbs, 31g Protein, 31g Fat, 477 Calories

Bacon Chicken Alfredo

Servings: 4
Cooking Time: 35 Minutes

Ingredients:
- 4-ounces mushrooms drained and sliced
- 1 cup shredded mozzarella cheese
- 1 jar Classico creamy alfredo sauce
- 6 slices chopped hickory bacon
- 4 boneless skinless chicken breasts thawed or fresh
- Pepper and salt to taste
- ½ cup water

Directions:
1. Add all ingredients in a pot on high fire and bring it to a boil.
2. Once boiling, lower fire to a simmer and cook for 30 minutes, stirring every now and then.
3. Adjust seasoning to taste.
4. Serve and enjoy.

Nutrition Info:
- Per Servings 7.7g Carbs, 75.8g Protein, 70.8g Fat, 976 Calories

Coconut Aminos Chicken Bake

Servings: 4
Cooking Time: 20 Minutes

Ingredients:
- 3 green onions, chopped
- 4 chicken breasts
- 4 oz. cheddar cheese, shredded
- 4 bacon strips
- 1 oz. coconut aminos
- 2 tbsp. coconut oil

Directions:
1. Heat oil in a skillet over high heat. Add chicken breasts and cook for 7 minutes both sides.
2. In another pan over medium-high heat, sauté bacon and place to a plate lined with a paper towel and crumble it.
3. Lay the chicken in a baking dish, sprinkle with coconut aminos, bacon, shredded cheese and chopped green onions.
4. Place the baking dish in the broiler and cook on High for 5 minutes. Serve and enjoy.

Nutrition Info:
- Per Servings 2g Carbs, 18g Protein, 49g Fat, 570 Calories

Quattro Formaggi Chicken

Servings: 8
Cooking Time: 40 Minutes

Ingredients:
- 3 pounds chicken breasts
- 2 ounces mozzarella cheese, cubed
- 2 ounces mascarpone cheese
- 4 ounces cheddar cheese, cubed
- 2 ounces provolone cheese, cubed
- 1 zucchini, shredded
- Salt and ground black pepper, to taste
- 1 tsp garlic, minced
- ½ cup pancetta, cooked and crumbled

Directions:
1. Sprinkle pepper and salt to the zucchini, squeeze well, and place to a bowl. Stir in the pancetta, mascarpone, cheddar cheese, provolone cheese, mozzarella, pepper, and garlic.
2. Cut slits into chicken breasts, apply pepper and salt, and stuff with the zucchini and cheese mixture. Set on a lined baking sheet, place in the oven at 400°F, and bake for 45 minutes.

Nutrition Info:
- Per Servings 2g Carbs, 51g Protein, 37g Fat, 565 Calories

Turkey & Leek Soup

Servings: 4
Cooking Time: 45 Minutes

Ingredients:
- 3 celery stalks, chopped
- 2 leeks, chopped
- 1 tbsp butter
- 6 cups chicken stock
- Salt and ground black pepper, to taste
- ¼ cup fresh parsley, chopped
- 3 cups zoodles
- 3 cups turkey meat, cooked and chopped

Directions:
1. Set a pot over medium-high heat, stir in leeks and celery and cook for 5 minutes. Place in the parsley, turkey meat, pepper, salt, and stock, and cook for 20 minutes. Stir in the zoodles, and cook turkey soup for 5 minutes. Serve in bowls and enjoy.

Nutrition Info:
- Per Servings 3g Carbs, 15g Protein, 11g Fat, 305 Calories

Greek Chicken With Capers

Servings: 4
Cooking Time: 30 Minutes

Ingredients:
- ¼ cup olive oil
- 1 onion, chopped
- 4 chicken breasts, skinless and boneless
- 4 garlic cloves, minced
- Salt and ground black pepper, to taste
- ½ cup kalamata olives, pitted and chopped
- 1 tbsp capers
- 1 pound tomatoes, chopped
- ½ tsp red chili flakes

Directions:
1. Sprinkle pepper and salt on the chicken, and rub with half of the oil. Add the chicken to a pan set over high heat, cook for 2 minutes, flip to the other side, and cook for 2 more minutes. Set the chicken breasts in the oven at 450ºF and bake for 8 minutes. Split the chicken into serving plates.
2. Set the same pan over medium heat and warm the remaining oil, place in the onion, olives, capers, garlic, and chili flakes, and cook for 1 minute. Stir in the tomatoes, pepper, and salt, and cook for 2 minutes. Sprinkle over the chicken breasts and enjoy.

Nutrition Info:
- Per Servings 2.2g Carbs, 25g Protein, 21g Fat, 387 Calories

Turkey Fajitas

Servings: 4
Cooking Time: 25 Minutes

Ingredients:
- 2 lb turkey breasts, skinless, boneless, sliced
- 1 tsp garlic powder
- 1 tsp chili powder
- 2 tsp cumin
- 2 tbsp lime juice
- Salt and black pepper, to taste
- 1 tsp sweet paprika
- 2 tbsp coconut oil
- 1 tsp ground coriander
- 1 green bell pepper, seeded, sliced
- 1 red bell pepper, seeded, sliced
- 1 onion, sliced
- 1 tbsp fresh cilantro, chopped
- 1 avocado, sliced
- 2 limes, cut into wedges

Directions:
1. Using a bowl, combine lime juice, cumin, garlic powder, coriander, paprika, salt, chili powder, and pepper. Toss in the turkey pieces to coat well. Set a pan over medium-high heat and warm oil, place in the turkey, cook each side for 3 minutes and set to a plate.
2. Add the remaining oil to the pan and warm over medium-high heat, stir in the bell peppers and onion, and cook for 6 minutes. Take the turkey back to the pan, add more seasonings if needed. Add a topping of fresh cilantro, lime wedges, and avocado and enjoy.

Nutrition Info:
- Per Servings 5g Carbs, 45g Protein, 32g Fat, 448 Calories

Easy Creamy Chicken

Servings: 8
Cooking Time: 15 Minutes

Ingredients:
- 5 tablespoons butter
- 2 cans crushed tomatoes
- 4 cooked chicken breasts, shredded
- 1 teaspoon herb seasoning mix of your choice
- ¼ cup parmesan cheese, grated
- Pepper and salt to taste

Directions:
1. Place a heavy-bottomed pot on medium-high fire and melt butter. Add tomatoes.
2. Sauté for 5 minutes, season with pepper, salt, and seasoning mix.
3. Stir in chicken. Mix well.
4. Cook until heated through, around 5 minutes.
5. Serve with a sprinkle of parmesan cheese.

Nutrition Info:
- Per Servings 2.3g Carbs, 29.5g Protein, 11.3g Fat, 235 Calories

Rosemary Turkey Pie

Servings: 4
Cooking Time: 40 Minutes

Ingredients:
- 2 cups chicken stock
- 1 cup turkey meat, cooked and chopped
- Salt and ground black pepper, to taste
- 1 tsp fresh rosemary, chopped
- ½ cup kale, chopped
- ½ cup butternut squash, chopped
- ½ cup Monterey jack cheese, shredded
- ¼ tsp smoked paprika
- ¼ tsp garlic powder
- ¼ tsp xanthan gum
- Cooking spray
- For the crust:
- ¼ cup butter
- ¼ tsp xanthan gum
- 2 cups almond flour
- A pinch of salt
- 1 egg
- ¼ cup cheddar cheese

Directions:
1. Set a greased pot over medium-high heat. Place in turkey and squash, and cook for 10 minutes. Stir in stock, Monterey Jack cheese, garlic powder, rosemary, pepper, smoked paprika, kale, and salt.
2. In a bowl, combine ½ cup stock from the pot with ¼ teaspoon xanthan gum, and transfer everything to the pot; set aside. In a separate bowl, stir together salt, ¼ teaspoon xanthan gum, and flour.
3. Stir in the butter, cheddar cheese, egg, until a pie crust dough forms. Form into a ball and refrigerate. Spray a baking dish with cooking spray and sprinkle pie filling on the bottom. Set the dough on a working surface, roll into a circle, and top filling with this. Ensure well pressed and seal edges, set in an oven at 350ºF, and bake for 35 minutes. Allow the pie to cool, and enjoy.

Nutrition Info:
- Per Servings 5.6g Carbs, 21g Protein, 23g Fat, 325 Calories

Roasted Chicken With Herbs

Servings: 12
Cooking Time: 50 Minutes

Ingredients:
- 1 whole chicken
- ½ tsp onion powder
- ½ tsp garlic powder
- Salt and black pepper, to taste
- 2 tbsp olive oil
- 1 tsp dry thyme
- 1 tsp dry rosemary
- 1 ½ cups chicken broth
- 2 tsp guar gum

Directions:
1. Rub the chicken with half of the oil, salt, rosemary, thyme, pepper, garlic powder, and onion powder. Place the rest of the oil into a baking dish, and add chicken. Place in the stock, and bake for 40 minutes. Remove the chicken to a platter, and set aside. Stir in the guar gum in a pan over medium heat, and cook until thickening. Place sauce over chicken to serve.

Nutrition Info:
- Per Servings 1.1g Carbs, 33g Protein, 15g Fat, 367 Calories

Thyme Chicken Thighs

Servings: 4
Cooking Time: 30 Minutes

Ingredients:
- ½ cup chicken stock
- 1 tbsp olive oil
- ½ cup chopped onion
- 4 chicken thighs
- ¼ cup heavy cream
- 2 tbsp Dijon mustard
- 1 tsp thyme
- 1 tsp garlic powder

Directions:
1. Heat the olive oil in a pan. Cook the chicken for about 4 minutes per side. Set aside. Sauté the onion in the same pan for 3 minutes, add the stock, and simmer for 5 minutes. Stir in mustard and heavy cream, along with thyme and garlic powder. Pour the sauce over the chicken and serve.

Nutrition Info:
- Per Servings 4g Carbs, 33g Protein, 42g Fat, 528 Calories

Chicken With Monterey Jack Cheese

Servings: 3
Cooking Time: 30 Minutes
Ingredients:
- 2 tbsp butter
- 1 tsp garlic, minced
- 1 pound chicken breasts
- 1 tsp creole seasoning
- ¼ cup scallions, chopped
- ½ cup tomatoes, chopped
- ½ cup chicken stock
- ¼ cup whipping cream
- ½ cup Monterey Jack cheese, grated
- ¼ cup fresh cilantro, chopped
- Salt and black pepper, to taste
- 4 ounces cream cheese
- 8 eggs
- A pinch of garlic powder

Directions:
1. Set a pan over medium heat and warm 1 tbsp butter. Add chicken, season with creole seasoning and cook each side for 2 minutes; remove to a plate. Melt the rest of the butter and stir in garlic and tomatoes; cook for 4 minutes. Return the chicken to the pan and pour in stock; cook for 15 minutes. Place in whipping cream, scallions, salt, Monterey Jack cheese, and pepper; cook for 2 minutes.
2. In a blender, combine the cream cheese with garlic powder, salt, eggs, and pepper, and pulse well. Place the mixture into a lined baking sheet, and then bake for 10 minutes in the oven at 325ºF. Allow the cheese sheet to cool down, place on a cutting board, roll, and slice into medium slices. Split the slices among bowls and top with chicken mixture. Sprinkle with chopped cilantro to serve.

Nutrition Info:
- Per Servings 4g Carbs, 39g Protein, 34g Fat, 445 Calories

Chicken & Squash Traybake

Servings: 4
Cooking Time: 60 Minutes
Ingredients:
- 2 lb chicken thighs
- 1 pound butternut squash, cubed
- ½ cup black olives, pitted
- ¼ cup olive oil
- 5 garlic cloves, sliced
- 1 tbsp dried oregano
- Salt and black pepper, to taste

Directions:
1. Set oven to 400ºF and grease a baking dish. Place in the chicken with the skin down. Set the garlic, olives and butternut squash around the chicken then drizzle with oil.
2. Spread pepper, salt, and oregano over the mixture then add into the oven. Cook for 45 minutes.

Nutrition Info:
- Per Servings 5.5g Carbs, 31g Protein, 15g Fat, 411 Calories

Smoky Paprika Chicken

Servings: 8
Cooking Time: 10 Minutes
Ingredients:
- 2 lb. chicken breasts, sliced into strips
- 2 tbsp. smoked paprika
- 1 tsp Cajun seasoning
- 1 tbsp minced garlic
- 1 large onion, sliced thinly
- Salt and pepper to taste
- 1 tbsp. olive oil

Directions:
1. In a large bowl, marinate chicken strips in paprika, Cajun, pepper, salt, and minced garlic for at least 30 minutes.
2. On high fire, heat a saucepan for 2 minutes. Add oil to the pan and swirl to coat bottom and sides. Heat oil for a minute.
3. Stir fry chicken and onion for 7 minutes or until chicken is cooked.
4. Serve and enjoy.

Nutrition Info:
- Per Servings 1.5g Carbs, 34g Protein, 12.4g Fat, 217 Calories

Chicken In Creamy Spinach Sauce

Servings: 4
Cooking Time: 20 Minutes

Ingredients:

- 1 pound chicken thighs
- 2 tbsp coconut oil
- 2 tbsp coconut flour
- 2 cups spinach, chopped
- 1 tsp oregano
- 1 cup heavy cream
- 1 cup chicken broth
- 2 tbsp butter

Directions:

1. Warm the coconut oil in a skillet and brown the chicken on all sides, about 6-8 minutes. Set aside.
2. Melt the butter and whisk in the flour over medium heat. Whisk in the heavy cream and chicken broth and bring to a boil. Stir in oregano. Add the spinach to the skillet and cook until wilted.
3. Add the thighs in the skillet and cook for an additional 5 minutes.

Nutrition Info:

- Per Servings 2.6g Carbs, 18g Protein, 38g Fat, 446 Calories

Easy Asian Chicken

Servings: 5
Cooking Time: 16 Minutes

Ingredients:

- 1 ½ lb. boneless chicken breasts, sliced into strips
- 1 tbsp ginger slices
- 3 tbsp coconut aminos
- ¼ cup organic chicken broth
- 3 cloves of garlic, minced
- 5 tablespoons sesame oil

Directions:

1. On high fire, heat a heavy-bottomed pot for 2 minutes. Add oil to a pan and swirl to coat bottom and sides. Heat oil for a minute.
2. Add garlic and ginger sauté for a minute.
3. Stir in chicken breast and sauté for 5 minutes. Season with coconut aminos and sauté for another 2 minutes.
4. Add remaining ingredients and bring to a boil.
5. Let it boil for 5 minutes.
6. Scrve and enjoy.

Nutrition Info:

- Per Servings 1.2g Carbs, 30.9g Protein, 17.6g Fat,

299 Calories

Sticky Cranberry Chicken Wings

Servings: 6
Cooking Time: 50 Minutes

Ingredients:

- 2 lb chicken wings
- 4 tbsp unsweetened cranberry puree
- 2 tbsp olive oil
- Salt to taste
- Sweet chili sauce to taste
- Lemon juice from 1 lemon

Directions:

1. Preheat the oven (broiler side) to 400°F. Then, in a bowl, mix the cranberry puree, olive oil, salt, sweet chili sauce, and lemon juice. After, add in the wings and toss to coat.
2. Place the chicken under the broiler, and cook for 45 minutes, turning once halfway.
3. Remove the chicken after and serve warm with a cranberry and cheese dipping sauce.

Nutrition Info:

- Per Servings 1.6g Carbs, 17.6g Protein, 8.5g Fat, 152 Calories

Chicken Curry

Servings: 6
Cooking Time: 30 Minutes

Ingredients:

- 1 ½ lb. boneless chicken breasts
- 2 tbsp. curry powder
- 2 cups chopped tomatoes
- 2 cups coconut milk, freshly squeezed
- 1 thumb-size ginger, peeled and sliced
- Pepper and salt to taste
- 2 tsp oil, divided

Directions:

1. On high fire, heat a saucepan for 2 minutes. Add 1 tsp oil to the pan and swirl to coat bottom and sides. Heat oil for a minute.
2. Sear chicken breasts for 4 minutes per side. Transfer to a chopping board and chop into bite-sized pieces.
3. Meanwhile, in the same pan, add remaining oil and heat for a minute. Add ginger sauté for a minute. Stir in tomatoes and curry powder. Crumble and wilt tomatoes for 5 minutes.
4. Add chopped chicken and continue sautéing for 7 minutes.

5. Deglaze the pot with 1 cup of coconut milk. Season with pepper and salt. Cover and simmer for 15 minutes.

6. Stir in remaining coconut milk and cook until heated through, around 3 minutes.

Nutrition Info:
- Per Servings 7.4g Carbs, 28.1g Protein, 22.4g Fat, 336 Calories

Turkey Burgers With Fried Brussels Sprouts

Servings: 4
Cooking Time: 30 Minutes

Ingredients:
- For the burgers
- 1 pound ground turkey
- 1 free-range egg
- ½ onion, chopped
- 1 tsp salt
- ½ tsp ground black pepper
- 1 tsp dried thyme
- 2 oz butter
- For the fried Brussels sprouts
- 1 ½ lb Brussels sprouts, halved
- 3 oz butter
- 1 tsp salt
- ½ tsp ground black pepper

Directions:
1. Combine the burger ingredients in a mixing bowl. Create patties from the mixture. Set a large pan over medium-high heat, warm butter, and fry the patties until cooked completely.
2. Place on a plate and cover with aluminium foil to keep warm. Fry brussels sprouts in butter, season to your preference, then set to a bowl. Plate the burgers and brussels sprouts and serve.

Nutrition Info:
- Per Servings 5.8g Carbs, 31g Protein, 25g Fat, 443 Calories

Chicken Gumbo

Servings: 5
Cooking Time: 40 Minutes

Ingredients:
- 2 sausages, sliced
- 3 chicken breasts, cubed
- 1 cup celery, chopped
- 2 tbsp dried oregano
- 2 bell peppers, seeded and chopped
- 1 onion, peeled and chopped
- 2 cups tomatoes, chopped
- 4 cups chicken broth
- 3 tbsp dried thyme
- 2 tbsp garlic powder
- 2 tbsp dry mustard
- 1 tsp cayenne powder
- 1 tbsp chili powder
- Salt and black pepper, to taste
- 6 tbsp cajun seasoning
- 3 tbsp olive oil

Directions:
1. In a pot over medium heat warm olive oil. Add the sausages, chicken, pepper, onion, dry mustard, chili, tomatoes, thyme, bell peppers, salt, oregano, garlic powder, cayenne, and cajun seasoning.
2. Cook for 10 minutes. Add the remaining ingredients and bring to a boil. Reduce the heat and simmer for 20 minutes covered. Serve hot divided between bowls.

Nutrition Info:
- Per Servings 6g Carbs, 26g Protein, 22g Fat, 361 Calories

Turkey & Cheese Stuffed Mushrooms

Servings: 5
Cooking Time: 20 Minutes

Ingredients:
- 12 ounces button mushroom caps
- 3 ounces cream cheese
- ¼ cup carrot, chopped
- 1 tsp ranch seasoning mix
- 4 tbsp hot sauce
- ¾ cup blue cheese, crumbled
- ¼ cup onion, chopped
- ½ cup turkey breasts, cooked, chopped
- Salt and black pepper, to taste
- Cooking spray

Directions:
1. Using a bowl, combine the cream cheese with the blue cheese, ranch seasoning, turkey, onion, carrot, salt, hot sauce, and pepper. Stuff each mushroom cap with this mixture, set on a lined baking sheet, spray with cooking spray, place in the oven at 425ºF, and bake for 10 minutes.

Nutrition Info:
- Per Servings 8.6g Carbs, 51g Protein, 17g Fat, 486 Calories

Chicken And Zucchini Bake

Servings: 4
Cooking Time: 45 Minutes

Ingredients:
- 1 zucchini, chopped
- Salt and black pepper, to taste
- 1 tsp garlic powder
- 1 tbsp avocado oil
- 2 chicken breasts, skinless, boneless, sliced
- 1 tomato, cored and chopped
- ½ tsp dried oregano
- ½ tsp dried basil
- ½ cup mozzarella cheese, shredded

Directions:
1. Apply pepper, garlic powder and salt to the chicken. Set a pan over medium heat and warm avocado oil, add in the chicken slices, cook until golden; remove to a baking dish. To the same pan add the zucchini, tomato, pepper, basil, oregano, and salt, cook for 2 minutes, and spread over chicken.
2. Bake in the oven at 330ºF for 20 minutes. Sprinkle the mozzarella over the chicken, return to the oven, and bake for 5 minutes until the cheese is melted and bubbling. Serve with green salad.

Nutrition Info:
- Per Servings 2g Carbs, 35g Protein, 11g Fat, 235 Calories

Spinach Chicken Cheesy Bake

Servings: 6
Cooking Time: 45 Minutes

Ingredients:
- 6 chicken breasts, skinless and boneless
- 1 tsp mixed spice seasoning
- Pink salt and black pepper to season
- 2 loose cups baby spinach
- 3 tsp olive oil
- 4 oz cream cheese, cubed
- 1 ¼ cups shredded mozzarella cheese
- 4 tbsp water

Directions:
1. Preheat oven to 370ºF.
2. Season chicken with spice mix, salt, and black pepper. Pat with your hands to have the seasoning stick on the chicken. Put in the casserole dish and layer spinach over the chicken. Mix the oil with cream cheese, mozzarella, salt, and black pepper and stir in water a tablespoon at a time. Pour the mixture over the chicken and

cover the pot with aluminium foil.
3. Bake for 20 minutes, remove foil and continue cooking for 15 minutes until a nice golden brown color is formed on top. Take out and allow sitting for 5 minutes.
4. Serve warm with braised asparagus.

Nutrition Info:
- Per Servings 3.1g Carbs, 15g Protein, 30.2g Fat, 340 Calories

Duck & Vegetable Casserole

Servings: 2
Cooking Time: 20 Minutes

Ingredients:
- 2 duck breasts, skin on and sliced
- 2 zucchinis, sliced
- 1 tbsp coconut oil
- 1 green onion bunch, chopped
- 1 carrot, chopped
- 2 green bell peppers, seeded and chopped
- Salt and ground black pepper, to taste

Directions:
1. Set a pan over medium-high heat and warm oil, stir in the green onions, and cook for 2 minutes. Place in the zucchini, bell peppers, pepper, salt, and carrot, and cook for 10 minutes.
2. Set another pan over medium-high heat, add in duck slices and cook each side for 3 minutes. Pour the mixture into the vegetable pan. Cook for 3 minutes. Set in bowls and enjoy.

Nutrition Info:
- Per Servings 8g Carbs, 53g Protein, 21g Fat, 433 Calories

Zucchini Spaghetti With Turkey Bolognese Sauce

Servings: 6
Cooking Time: 30 Minutes

Ingredients:
- 2 cups sliced mushrooms
- 2 tsp olive oil
- 1 pound ground turkey
- 3 tbsp pesto sauce
- 1 cup diced onion
- 2 cups broccoli florets
- 6 cups zucchini, spiralized

Directions:
1. Heat the oil in a skillet. Add zucchini and cook for

2-3 minutes, stirring continuously; set aside.

2. Add turkey to the skillet and cook until browned, about 7-8 minutes. Transfer to a plate. Add onion and cook until translucent, about 3 minutes. Add broccoli and mushrooms, and cook for 7 more minutes. Return the turkey to the skillet. Stir in the pesto sauce. Cover the pan, lower the heat, and simmer for 15 minutes. Stir in zucchini pasta and serve immediately.

Nutrition Info:

• Per Servings 3.8g Carbs, 19g Protein, 16g Fat, 273 Calories

Easy Bbq Chicken And Cheese

Servings: 4

Cooking Time: 40 Minutes

Ingredients:

• 1-pound chicken tenders, boneless
• ½ cup commercial BBQ sauce, keto-friendly
• 1 teaspoon liquid smoke
• 1 cup mozzarella cheese, grated
• ½ pound bacon, fried and crumbled
• Pepper and salt to taste

Directions:

1. With paper towels, dry chicken tenders. Season with pepper and salt.
2. Place chicken tenders on an oven-safe dish.
3. Whisk well BBQ sauce and liquid smoke in a bowl and pour over chicken tenders. Coat well in the sauce.
4. Bake in a preheated 400oF oven for 30 minutes.
5. Remove from oven, turnover chicken tenders, sprinkle cheese on top.
6. Return to the oven and continue baking for 10 minutes more.
7. Serve and enjoy with a sprinkle of bacon bits.

Nutrition Info:

• Per Servings 6.7g Carbs, 34.6g Protein, 31.5g Fat, 351 Calories

Coconut Chicken Soup

Servings: 4

Cooking Time: 30 Minutes

Ingredients:

• 3 tbsp butter
• 4 ounces cream cheese
• 2 chicken breasts, diced
• 4 cups chicken stock
• Salt and black pepper, to taste
• ½ cup coconut cream
• ¼ cup celery, chopped

Directions:

1. In the blender, combine stock, butter, coconut cream, salt, cream cheese, and pepper. Remove to a pot, heat over medium heat, and stir in the chicken and celery. Simmer for 15 minutes, separate into bowls, and enjoy.

Nutrition Info:

• Per Servings 5g Carbs, 31g Protein, 23g Fat, 387 Calories

Chicken With Asparagus & Root Vegetables

Servings: 4

Cooking Time: 35 Minutes

Ingredients:

• 2 cups whipping cream
• 3 chicken breasts, boneless, skinless, chopped
• 3 tbsp butter
• ½ cup onion, chopped
• ¾ cup carrot, chopped
• 5 cups chicken stock
• Salt and black pepper, to taste
• 1 bay leaf
• 1 turnip, chopped
• 1 parsnip, chopped
• 17 ounces asparagus, trimmed
• 3 tsp fresh thyme, chopped

Directions:

1. Set a pan over medium heat and add whipping cream, allow simmering, and cook until it's reduced by half for about 7 minutes. Set another pan over medium heat and warm butter, sauté the onion for 3 minutes. Pour in the chicken stock, carrots, turnip, and parsnip, chicken, and bay leaf, bring to a boil, and simmer for 20 minutes.
2. Add in the asparagus and cook for 7 minutes. Discard the bay leaf, stir in the reduced whipping cream, adjust the seasoning and ladle the stew into serving bowls. Scatter with fresh thyme.

Nutrition Info:

• Per Servings 7.4g Carbs, 37g Protein, 31g Fat, 497 Calories

Garlic & Ginger Chicken With Peanut Sauce

Servings: 6
Cooking Time: 1 Hour And 50 Minutes
Ingredients:
- 1 tbsp wheat-free soy sauce
- 1 tbsp sugar-free fish sauce
- 1 tbsp lime juice
- 1 tsp cilantro
- 1 tsp minced garlic
- 1 tsp minced ginger
- 1 tbsp olive oil
- 1 tbsp rice wine vinegar
- 1 tsp cayenne pepper
- 1 tsp erythritol
- 6 chicken thighs
- Sauce:
- ½ cup peanut butter
- 1 tsp minced garlic
- 1 tbsp lime juice
- 2 tbsp water
- 1 tsp minced ginger
- 1 tbsp chopped jalapeño
- 2 tbsp rice wine vinegar
- 2 tbsp erythritol
- 1 tbsp fish sauce

Directions:
1. Combine all chicken ingredients in a large Ziploc bag. Seal the bag and shake to combine. Refrigerate for 1 hour. Remove from fridge about 15 minutes before cooking.
2. Preheat the grill to medium and grill the chicken for 7 minutes per side. Whisk together all sauce ingredients in a mixing bowl. Serve the chicken drizzled with peanut sauce.

Nutrition Info:
- Per Servings 3g Carbs, 35g Protein, 36g Fat, 492 Calories

Chicken Pesto

Servings: 8
Cooking Time: 35 Minutes
Ingredients:
- 5 cloves of garlic
- 4 skinless, boneless chicken breast halves, cut into thin strips
- 3 tbsp grated Parmesan cheese
- ¼ cup pesto

- 1 ¼ cups heavy cream
- 10 tbsps olive oil
- Pepper to taste
- 1/8 tsp salt

Directions:
1. On medium fire, place a large saucepan and heat olive oil.
2. Add garlic and chicken, sauté for 7 minutes, or until chicken strips are nearly cooked.
3. Lower fire and add Parmesan cheese, pesto, cream, pepper, and salt.
4. Continue cooking for 5-10 minutes more or until chicken is fully cooked. Stir frequently.
5. Once penne is cooked, drain well and pour into a large saucepan, toss to coat, and serve.

Nutrition Info:
- Per Servings 3g Carbs, 30.0g Protein, 22.0g Fat, 330 Calories

Roast Chicken With Herb Stuffing

Servings: 8
Cooking Time: 120 Minutes
Ingredients:
- 5-pound whole chicken
- 1 bunch oregano
- 1 bunch thyme
- 1 tbsp marjoram
- 1 tbsp parsley
- 1 tbsp olive oil
- 2 pounds Brussels sprouts
- 1 lemon
- 4 tbsp butter

Directions:
1. Preheat your oven to 450ºF.
2. Stuff the chicken with oregano, thyme, and lemon. Make sure the wings are tucked over and behind.
3. Roast for 15 minutes. Reduce the heat to 325ºF and cook for 40 minutes. Spread the butter over the chicken, and sprinkle parsley and marjoram. Add the brussels sprouts. Return to the oven and bake for 40 more minutes. Let sit for 10 minutes before carving.

Nutrition Info:
- Per Servings 5.1g Carbs, 30g Protein, 32g Fat, 432 Calories

Soups, Stew & Salads Recipes

Soups, Stew & Salads Recipes

Asparagus Niçoise Salad

Servings: 4
Cooking Time: 0 Minutes

Ingredients:
- 1-pound fresh asparagus, trimmed and blanched
- 2 ½ ounces white tuna in oil
- ½ cup pitted Greek olives, halved
- ½ cup zesty Italian salad dressing
- Salt and pepper to taste
- 3 tablespoons olive oil

Directions:
1. Place all ingredients in a bowl.
2. Toss to mix all ingredients.
3. Serve.

Nutrition Info:
- Per Servings 10g Carbs, 8g Protein, 20g Fat, 239 Calories

Tuna Salad With Lettuce & Olives

Servings: 2
Cooking Time: 5 Minutes

Ingredients:
- 1 cup canned tuna, drained
- 1 tsp onion flakes
- 3 tbsp mayonnaise
- 1 cup shredded romaine lettuce
- 1 tbsp lime juice
- Sea salt, to taste
- 6 black olives, pitted and sliced

Directions:
1. Combine the tuna, mayonnaise, lime juice, and salt in a small bowl; mix to combine well. In a salad platter, arrange the shredded lettuce and onion flakes. Spread the tuna mixture over; top with black olives to serve.

Nutrition Info:
- Per Servings 2g Carbs, 18.5g Protein, 20g Fat, 248 Calories

Chicken And Cauliflower Rice Soup

Servings: 8
Cooking Time: 20 Mins

Ingredients:
- 2 cooked, boneless chicken breast halves, shredded
- 2 packages Steamed Cauliflower Rice
- 1/4 cup celery, chopped
- 1/2 cup onion, chopped
- 4 garlic cloves, minced
- Salt and ground black pepper to taste
- 2 teaspoons poultry seasoning
- 4 cups chicken broth
- ½ cup butter
- 2 cups heavy cream

Directions:
1. Heat butter in a large pot over medium heat, add onion, celery and garlic cloves to cook until tender. Meanwhile, place the riced cauliflower steam bags in the microwave following directions on the package.
2. Add the riced cauliflower, seasoning, salt and black pepper to butter mixture, saute them for 7 minutes on medium heat, stirring constantly to well combined.
3. Bring cooked chicken breast halves, broth and heavy cream to a broil. When it starts boiling, lower the heat, cover and simmer for 15 minutes.

Nutrition Info:
- Per Servings 6g Carbs, 27g Protein, 30g Fat, 415 Calories

Citrusy Brussels Sprouts Salad

Servings: 6
Cooking Time: 3 Minutes

Ingredients:
- 2 tablespoons olive oil
- ¾ pound Brussels sprouts
- 1 cup walnuts
- Juice from 1 lemon
- ½ cup grated parmesan cheese
- Salt and pepper to taste

Directions:
1. Heat oil in a skillet over medium flame and sauté the Brussels sprouts for 3 minutes until slightly wilted. Removed from heat and allow to cool.

2. In a bowl, toss together the cooled Brussels sprouts and the rest of the ingredients.

3. Toss to coat.

Nutrition Info:
- Per Servings 8g Carbs, 6g Protein, 23g Fat, 259 Calories

Green Salad

Servings: 4
Cooking Time: 30 Minutes

Ingredients:
- 2 cups green beans, chopped
- 2 cups shredded spinach
- ½ cup parmesan cheese
- 3 cups basil leaves
- 3 cloves of garlic
- Salt to taste
- ¼ cup olive oil

Directions:
1. Heat a little olive oil in a skillet over medium heat and add the green beans and season with salt to taste. Sauté for 3 to 5 minutes.

2. Place the green beans in a bowl and add in the spinach.

3. In a food processor, combine half of the parmesan cheese, basil, and garlic. Add in the rest of the oil and season with salt and pepper to taste.

4. Pour into the green beans and toss to coat the ingredients.

Nutrition Info:
- Per Servings 6g Carbs, 5g Protein, 17g Fat, 196 Calories

Broccoli Slaw Salad With Mustard-mayo Dressing

Servings: 6
Cooking Time: 10 Minutes

Ingredients:
- 2 tbsp granulated swerve
- 1 tbsp Dijon mustard
- 1 tbsp olive oil
- 4 cups broccoli slaw
- ⅓ cup mayonnaise, sugar-free
- 1 tsp celery seeds
- 1 ½ tbsp apple cider vinegar
- Salt and black pepper, to taste

Directions:
1. Whisk together all ingredients except the broccoli slaw. Place broccoli slaw in a large salad bowl. Pour the dressing over. Mix with your hands to combine well.

Nutrition Info:
- Per Servings 2g Carbs, 3g Protein, 10g Fat, 110 Calories

Cobb Egg Salad In Lettuce Cups

Servings: 4
Cooking Time: 20 Minutes

Ingredients:
- 2 chicken breasts, cut into pieces
- 1 tbsp olive oil
- Salt and black pepper to season
- 6 large eggs
- 1 ½ cups water
- 2 tomatoes, seeded, chopped
- 6 tbsp Greek yogurt
- 1 head green lettuce, firm leaves removed for cups

Directions:
1. Preheat oven to 400°F. Put the chicken pieces in a bowl, drizzle with olive oil, and sprinkle with salt and black pepper. Mix the ingredients until the chicken is well coated with the seasoning.

2. Put the chicken on a prepared baking sheet and spread out evenly. Slide the baking sheet in the oven and bake the chicken until cooked through and golden brown for 8 minutes, turning once.

3. Bring the eggs to boil in salted water in a pot over medium heat for 6 minutes. Run the eggs in cold water, peel, and chop into small pieces. Transfer to a salad bowl.

4. Remove the chicken from the oven when ready and add to the salad bowl. Include the tomatoes and Greek yogurt; mix evenly with a spoon. Layer two lettuce leaves each as cups and fill with two tablespoons of egg salad each. Serve with chilled blueberry juice.

Nutrition Info:
- Per Servings 4g Carbs, 21g Protein, 24.5g Fat, 325 Calories

Thyme & Wild Mushroom Soup

Servings: 4
Cooking Time: 25 Minutes

Ingredients:
- ¼ cup butter
- ½ cup crème fraiche
- 12 oz wild mushrooms, chopped
- 2 tsp thyme leaves
- 2 garlic cloves, minced
- 4 cups chicken broth
- Salt and black pepper, to taste

Directions:
1. Melt the butter in a large pot over medium heat. Add garlic and cook for one minute until tender. Add mushrooms, salt and pepper, and cook for 10 minutes. Pour the broth over and bring to a boil.
2. Reduce the heat and simmer for 10 minutes. Puree the soup with a hand blender until smooth. Stir in crème Fraiche. Garnish with thyme leaves before serving.

Nutrition Info:
- Per Servings 5.8g Carbs, 6.1g Protein, 25g Fat, 281 Calories

Pumpkin & Meat Peanut Stew

Servings: 6
Cooking Time: 45 Minutes

Ingredients:
- 1 cup pumpkin puree
- 2 pounds chopped pork stew meat
- 1 tbsp peanut butter
- 4 tbsp chopped peanuts
- 1 garlic clove, minced
- ½ cup chopped onion
- ½ cup white wine
- 1 tbsp olive oil
- 1 tsp lemon juice
- ¼ cup granulated sweetener
- ¼ tsp cardamom
- ¼ tsp allspice
- 2 cups water
- 2 cups chicken stock

Directions:
1. Heat the olive oil in a large pot and sauté onion for 3 minutes, until translucent. Add garlic and cook for 30 more seconds. Add the pork and cook until browned, about 5-6 minutes, stirring occasionally. Pour in the wine and cook for one minute.

2. Add in the remaining ingredients, except for the lemon juice and peanuts. Bring the mixture to a boil, and cook for 5 minutes. Reduce the heat to low, cover the pot, and let cook for about 30 minutes. Adjust seasoning and stir in the lemon juice before serving.
3. Ladle into serving bowls and serve topped with peanuts.

Nutrition Info:
- Per Servings 4g Carbs, 27.5g Protein, 33g Fat, 451 Calories

Fruit Salad With Poppy Seeds

Servings: 5
Cooking Time: 25 Mins

Ingredients:
- 1 tablespoon poppy seeds
- 1 head romaine lettuce, torn into bite-size pieces
- 4 ounces shredded Swiss cheese
- 1 avocado- peeled, cored and diced
- 2 teaspoons diced onion
- 1/2 cup lemon juice
- 1/2 cup stevia
- 1/2 teaspoon salt
- 2/3 cup olive oil
- 1 teaspoon Dijon style prepared mustard

Directions:
1. Combine stevia, lemon juice, onion, mustard, and salt in a blender. Process until well blended.
2. Add oil until mixture is thick and smooth. Add poppy seeds, stir just a few seconds or more to mix.
3. In a large serving bowl, toss together the remaining ingredients.
4. Pour dressing over salad just before serving, and toss to coat.

Nutrition Info:
- Per Servings 6g Carbs, 4.9g Protein, 20.6g Fat, 277 Calories

Caesar Salad With Smoked Salmon And Poached Eggs

Servings: 4
Cooking Time: 15 Minutes

Ingredients:
- 3 cups water
- 8 eggs
- 2 cups torn romaine lettuce
- ½ cup smoked salmon, chopped
- 6 slices bacon

• 2 tbsp Heinz low carb Caesar dressing

Directions:

1. Boil the water in a pot over medium heat for 5 minutes and bring to simmer. Crack each egg into a small bowl and gently slide into the water. Poach for 2 to 3 minutes, remove with a perforated spoon, transfer to a paper towel to dry, and plate. Poach the remaining 7 eggs.

2. Put the bacon in a skillet and fry over medium heat until browned and crispy, about 6 minutes, turning once. Remove, allow cooling, and chop in small pieces.

3. Toss the lettuce, smoked salmon, bacon, and caesar dressing in a salad bowl. Divide the salad into 4 plates, top with two eggs each, and serve immediately or chilled.

Nutrition Info:

• Per Servings 5g Carbs, 8g Protein, 21g Fat, 260 Calories

Spinach Fruit Salad With Seeds

Servings: 4

Cooking Time: 1 Hour 10 Minutes

Ingredients:

• 2 tablespoons sesame seeds
• 1 tablespoon poppy seeds
• 1 tablespoon minced onion
• 10 ounces fresh spinach - rinsed, dried and torn into bite-size pieces
• 1 quart strawberries - cleaned, hulled and sliced
• 1/2 cup stevia
• 1/2 cup olive oil
• 1/4 cup distilled white vinegar
• 1/4 teaspoon Worcestershire sauce
• 1/4 teaspoon paprika

Directions:

1. Mix together the spinach and strawberry in a large bowl, stir in the sesame seeds, poppy seeds, stevia, olive oil, vinegar, paprika, Worcestershire sauce and onion in a medium bowl. Cover and cool for 1 hour.

2. Pour dressing over salad to combine well. Serve immediately or refrigerate for 15 minutes.

Nutrition Info:

• Per Servings 8.6g Carbs, 6g Protein, 18g Fat, 220 Calories

Cream Of Thyme Tomato Soup

Servings: 6

Cooking Time: 20 Minutes

Ingredients:

• 2 tbsp ghee
• 2 large red onions, diced
• ½ cup raw cashew nuts, diced
• 2 cans tomatoes
• 1 tsp fresh thyme leaves + extra to garnish
• 1 ½ cups water
• Salt and black pepper to taste
• 1 cup heavy cream

Directions:

1. Melt ghee in a pot over medium heat and sauté the onions for 4 minutes until softened.

2. Stir in the tomatoes, thyme, water, cashews, and season with salt and black pepper. Cover and bring to simmer for 10 minutes until thoroughly cooked.

3. Open, turn the heat off, and puree the ingredients with an immersion blender. Adjust to taste and stir in the heavy cream. Spoon into soup bowls and serve with low carb parmesan cheese toasts.

Nutrition Info:

• Per Servings 3g Carbs, 11g Protein, 27g Fat, 310 Calories

Creamy Soup With Greens

Servings: 6

Cooking Time: 20 Minutes

Ingredients:

• ½-pounds collard greens, torn to bite-sized pieces
• 5 cups chicken broth
• 2 cups broccoli florets
• 1 cup diced onion
• 3 tablespoon oil
• 4 tablespoons butter
• Salt and pepper to taste

Directions:

1. Add all ingredients to the pot and bring to a boil.

2. Lower fire to a simmer and simmer for 15 minutes while covered.

3. With an immersion blender, puree soup until creamy.

4. Adjust seasoning to taste.

5. Serve and enjoy.

Nutrition Info:

• Per Servings 6.5g Carbs, 50.6g Protein, 33.5g Fat, 548 Calories

Chicken Cabbage Soup

Servings: 6
Cooking Time: 30 Minutes

Ingredients:
- 1 can Italian-style tomatoes
- 3 cups chicken broth
- 1 chicken breast
- ½ head of cabbage, shredded
- 1 packet Italian seasoning mix
- Salt and pepper to taste
- 1 cup water
- 1 tsp oil

Directions:
1. Place a heavy-bottomed pot on medium fire and heat for a minute. Add oil and swirl to coat the bottom and sides of the pot.
2. Pan fry chicken breast for 4 minutes per side. Transfer to a chopping board and cut into ½-inch cubes.
3. Add all ingredients to the pot and stir well.
4. Cover and bring to a boil, lower fire to a simmer, and cook for 20 minutes.
5. Adjust seasoning to taste, serve, and enjoy.

Nutrition Info:
- Per Servings 5.6g Carbs, 34.1g Protein, 9.3g Fat, 248 Calories

Bacon And Spinach Salad

Servings: 4
Cooking Time: 20 Minutes

Ingredients:
- 2 large avocados, 1 chopped and 1 sliced
- 1 spring onion, sliced
- 4 cooked bacon slices, crumbled
- 2 cups spinach
- 2 small lettuce heads, chopped
- 2 hard-boiled eggs, chopped
- Vinaigrette:
- 3 tbsp olive oil
- 1 tsp Dijon mustard
- 1 tbsp apple cider vinegar

Directions:
1. Combine the spinach, lettuce, eggs, chopped avocado, and spring onion, in a large bowl. Whisk together the vinaigrette ingredients in another bowl.
2. Pour the dressing over, toss to combine and top with the sliced avocado and bacon.

Nutrition Info:
- Per Servings 3.4g Carbs, 7g Protein, 33g Fat, 350 Calories

Mushroom-broccoli Soup

Servings: 4
Cooking Time: 20 Minutes

Ingredients:
- 1 onion, diced
- 3 cloves of garlic, diced
- 2 cups mushrooms, chopped
- 2 heads of broccoli, cut into florets
- 1 cup full-fat milk
- 3 cups water
- Pepper and salt to taste

Directions:
1. Place a heavy-bottomed pot on medium-high fire and heat for 3 minutes.
2. Add onion, garlic, water, and broccoli. Season generously with pepper and salt.
3. Cover and bring to a boil. Once boiling, lower fire to a simmer and let it cook for 7 minutes.
4. With a handheld blender, puree mixture until smooth and creamy.
5. Stir in mushrooms and milk, cover, and simmer for another 8 minutes.
6. Serve and enjoy.

Nutrition Info:
- Per Servings 8.5g Carbs, 3.8g Protein, 1.0g Fat, 58.2 Calories

Watermelon And Cucumber Salad

Servings: 10
Cooking Time: 0 Minutes

Ingredients:
- ½ large watermelon, diced
- 1 cucumber, peeled and diced
- 1 red onion, chopped
- ¼ cup feta cheese
- ½ cup heavy cream
- Salt to taste
- 5 tbsp MCT or coconut oil

Directions:
1. Place all ingredients in a bowl.
2. Toss everything to coat.
3. Place in the fridge to cool before serving.

Nutrition Info:
- Per Servings 2.5g Carbs, 0.9g Protein, 100g Fat, 910 Calories

Bacon Chowder

Servings: 6
Cooking Time: 15 Minutes
Ingredients:
- 1-pound bacon strips, chopped
- 1/4 cup chopped onion
- 1 can evaporated milk
- 1 sprig parsley, chopped
- 5 tablespoons butter
- 1/4 teaspoon salt
- 1/4 teaspoon pepper

Directions:

1. In a large skillet, cook bacon over medium heat until crisp, stirring occasionally. Remove with a slotted spoon; drain on paper towels. Discard drippings, reserving 1-1/2 teaspoons in the pan. Add onion to drippings; cook and stir over medium-high heat until tender.
2. Meanwhile, place all ingredients Bring to a boil over high heat. Reduce heat to medium; cook, uncovered, 10-15 minutes or until tender. Reserve 1 cup potato water.
3. Add milk, salt and pepper to the saucepan; heat through. Stir in bacon and onion.

Nutrition Info:
- Per Servings 5.4g Carbs, 10g Protein, 31.9g Fat, 322 Calories

Kale And Brussels Sprouts

Servings: 6
Cooking Time: 0 Minutes
Ingredients:
- 1 small bunch kale, thinly sliced
- ½ pound fresh Brussels sprouts, thinly sliced
- ½ cup pistachios, chopped coarsely
- ½ cup honey mustard salad dressing
- ¼ cup parmesan cheese, shredded
- Salt and pepper to taste

Directions:
1. Place all ingredients in a salad bowl.
2. Toss to coat everything.
3. Serve.

Nutrition Info:
- Per Servings 9g Carbs, 5g Protein, 15g Fat, 198 Calories

Mushroom Soup

Servings: 8
Cooking Time: 35 Minutes
Ingredients:
- 1-pound baby portobello mushrooms, chopped
- 2 tablespoons olive oil
- 1 carton reduced-sodium beef broth
- 2 cups heavy whipping cream
- 4 tablespoons butter
- 1/2 cup water

Directions:
1. In a Dutch oven, sauté mushrooms in oil and butter until tender.
2. Add the contents of seasoning packets, broth, and water. Bring to a boil.
3. Reduce heat; cover and simmer for 25 minutes.
4. Add cream and heat through.

Nutrition Info:
- Per Servings 3.6g Carbs, 8g Protein, 26g Fat, 280 Calories

Pesto Tomato Cucumber Salad

Servings: 8
Cooking Time: 0 Minutes
Ingredients:
- ½ cup Italian salad dressing
- ¼ cup prepared pesto
- 3 large tomatoes, sliced
- 2 medium cucumbers, halved and sliced
- 1 small red onion, sliced
- Salt and pepper to taste
- 3 tablespoons olive oil

Directions:
1. In a bowl, whisk the salad dressing and pesto. Season with salt and pepper to taste.
2. Toss gently to incorporate everything.
3. Refrigerate before serving.

Nutrition Info:
- Per Servings 3.7g Carbs, 1.8g Protein, 12g Fat, 128 Calories

Easy Tomato Salad

Servings: 4
Cooking Time: 0 Minutes

Ingredients:
- 1 ½ cups cherry tomatoes, sliced
- ¼ cup white wine vinegar
- 1/8 cup chives
- 3 tablespoons olive oil
- Salt and pepper to taste

Directions:
1. Put all ingredients in a bowl.
2. Toss to combine.
3. Serve immediately.

Nutrition Info:
- Per Servings 0.6g Carbs, 0.3g Protein, 10.1g Fat, 95 Calories

Beef Reuben Soup

Servings: 6
Cooking Time: 20 Minutes

Ingredients:
- 1 onion, diced
- 6 cups beef stock
- 1 tsp caraway seeds
- 2 celery stalks, diced
- 2 garlic cloves, minced
- 2 cups heavy cream
- 1 cup sauerkraut
- 1 pound corned beef, chopped
- 3 tbsp butter
- 1 ½ cup swiss cheese
- Salt and black pepper, to taste

Directions:
1. Melt the butter in a large pot. Add onion and celery, and fry for 3 minutes until tender. Add garlic and cook for another minute.
2. Pour the beef stock over and stir in sauerkraut, salt, caraway seeds, and add a pinch of pepper. Bring to a boil. Reduce the heat to low, and add the corned beef. Cook for about 15 minutes, adjust the seasoning. Stir in heavy cream and cheese and cook for 1 minute.

Nutrition Info:
- Per Servings 8g Carbs, 23g Protein, 37g Fat, 450 Calories

Spicy Chicken Bean Soup

Servings: 8
Cooking Time:1h 20 Mins

Ingredients:
- 8 skinless, boneless chicken breast halves
- 5 cubes chicken bouillon
- 2 cans peeled and diced tomatoes
- 1 container sour cream
- 1 cups frozen cut green beans
- 3 tablespoons. olive oil
- Salt and black pepper to taste
- 1 onion, chopped
- 3 cloves garlic, chopped
- 1 cups frozen cut green beans

Directions:
1. Heat olive oil in a large pot over medium heat, add onion, garlic and cook until tender. Stir in water, chicken, salt, pepper, bouillon cubes and bring to boil, simmer for 1 hour on Low. Remove chicken from the pot, reserve 5 cups broth and slice.
2. Stir in the remaining ingredients in the pot and simmer 30 minutes. Serve and enjoy.

Nutrition Info:
- Per Servings 7.6g Carbs, 26.5g Protein, 15.3g Fat, 275.1 Calories

Insalata Caprese

Servings: 8
Cooking Time: 0 Minutes

Ingredients:
- 2 ½ pounds tomatoes, cut into 1-in pieces
- 8 ounces mozzarella cheese pearls
- ½ cup ripe olives, pitted
- ¼ cup fresh basil, sliced thinly
- Balsamic vinegar (optional)
- Salt and pepper to taste
- 3 tablespoons olive oil

Directions:
1. Place all ingredients in a bowl.
2. Season with salt and pepper to taste. Drizzle with balsamic vinegar if available.
3. Toss to coat.
4. Serve immediately.

Nutrition Info:
- Per Servings 7g Carbs, 6g Protein, 12g Fat, 160 Calories

Green Mackerel Salad

Servings: 2
Cooking Time: 25 Minutes

Ingredients:

- 2 mackerel fillets
- 2 hard-boiled eggs, sliced
- 1 tbsp coconut oil
- 2 cups green beans
- 1 avocado, sliced
- 4 cups mixed salad greens
- 2 tbsp olive oil
- 2 tbsp lemon juice
- 1 tsp Dijon mustard
- Salt and black pepper, to taste

Directions:

1. Fill a saucepan with water and add the green beans and salt. Cook over medium heat for about 3 minutes. Drain and set aside.
2. Melt the coconut oil in a pan over medium heat. Add the mackerel fillets and cook for about 4 minutes per side, or until opaque and crispy. Divide the green beans between two salad bowls. Top with mackerel, egg, and avocado slices.
3. In a bowl, whisk together the lemon juice, olive oil, mustard, salt, and pepper, and drizzle over the salad.

Nutrition Info:

- Per Servings 7.6g Carbs, 27.3g Protein, 41.9g Fat, 525 Calories

Brazilian Moqueca (shrimp Stew)

Servings: 6
Cooking Time: 25 Minutes

Ingredients:

- 1 cup coconut milk
- 2 tbsp lime juice
- ¼ cup diced roasted peppers
- 1 ½ pounds shrimp, peeled and deveined
- ¼ cup olive oil
- 1 garlic clove, minced
- 14 ounces diced tomatoes
- 2 tbsp sriracha sauce
- 1 chopped onion
- ¼ cup chopped cilantro
- Fresh dill, chopped to garnish
- Salt and black pepper, to taste

Directions:

1. Heat the olive oil in a pot over medium heat. Add onion and cook for 3 minutes or until translucent. Add the garlic and cook for another minute, until soft. Add tomatoes, shrimp, and cilantro. Cook until the shrimp becomes opaque, about 3-4 minutes.
2. Stir in sriracha sauce and coconut milk, and cook for 2 minutes. Do not bring to a boil. Stir in the lime juice and season with salt and pepper. Spoon the stew in bowls, garnish with fresh dill to serve.

Nutrition Info:

- Per Servings 5g Carbs, 23.1g Protein, 21g Fat, 324 Calories

Creamy Cauliflower Soup With Chorizo Sausage

Servings: 4
Cooking Time: 40 Minutes

Ingredients:

- 1 cauliflower head, chopped
- 1 turnip, chopped
- 3 tbsp butter
- 1 chorizo sausage, sliced
- 2 cups chicken broth
- 1 small onion, chopped
- 2 cups water
- Salt and black pepper, to taste

Directions:

1. Melt 2 tbsp. of the butter in a large pot over medium heat. Stir in onion and cook until soft and golden, about 3-4 minutes. Add cauliflower and turnip, and cook for another 5 minutes.
2. Pour the broth and water over. Bring to a boil, simmer covered, and cook for about 20 minutes until the vegetables are tender. Remove from heat. Melt the remaining butter in a skillet. Add the chorizo sausage and cook for 5 minutes until crispy. Puree the soup with a hand blender until smooth. Taste and adjust the seasonings. Serve the soup in deep bowls topped with the chorizo sausage.

Nutrition Info:

- Per Servings 5.7g Carbs, 10g Protein, 19.1g Fat, 251 Calories

Broccoli Cheese Soup

Servings: 4
Cooking Time: 20 Minutes

Ingredients:
- ¾ cup heavy cream
- 1 onion, diced
- 1 tsp minced garlic
- 4 cups chopped broccoli
- 4 cups veggie broth
- 2 tbsp butter
- 2 ¾ cups grated cheddar cheese
- ¼ cup cheddar cheese to garnish
- Salt and black pepper, to taste
- ½ bunch fresh mint, chopped

Directions:
1. Melt the butter in a large pot over medium heat. Sauté onion and garlic for 3 minutes or until tender, stirring occasionally. Season with salt and pepper. Add the broth, broccoli and bring to a boil.
2. Reduce the heat and simmer for 10 minutes. Puree the soup with a hand blender until smooth. Add in the cheese and cook about 1 minute. Taste, season with salt and pepper. Stir in the heavy cream.Serve in bowls with the reserved grated Cheddar cheese and sprinkled with fresh mint.

Nutrition Info:
- Per Servings 7g Carbs, 23.8g Protein, 52.3g Fat, 561 Calories

Salsa Verde Chicken Soup

Servings: 4
Cooking Time: 15 Minutes

Ingredients:
- ½ cup salsa verde
- 2 cups cooked and shredded chicken
- 2 cups chicken broth
- 1 cup shredded cheddar cheese
- 4 ounces cream cheese
- ½ tsp chili powder
- ½ tsp ground cumin
- ½ tsp fresh cilantro, chopped
- Salt and black pepper, to taste

Directions:
1. Combine the cream cheese, salsa verde, and broth, in a food processor; pulse until smooth. Transfer the mixture to a pot and place over medium heat. Cook until hot, but do not bring to a boil.
2. Add chicken, chili powder, and cumin and cook for about 3-5 minutes, or until it is heated through.
3. Stir in Cheddar cheese and season with salt and pepper to taste. If it is very thick, add a few tablespoons of water and boil for 1-3 more minutes. Serve hot in bowls sprinkled with fresh cilantro.

Nutrition Info:
- Per Servings 3g Carbs, 25g Protein, 23g Fat, 346 Calories

Arugula Prawn Salad With Mayo Dressing

Servings: 4
Cooking Time: 15 Minutes

Ingredients:
- 4 cups baby arugula
- ½ cup garlic mayonnaise
- 3 tbsp olive oil
- 1 lb tiger prawns, peeled and deveined
- 1 tsp Dijon mustard
- Salt and chili pepper to season
- 2 tbsp lemon juice

Directions:
1. Add the mayonnaise, lemon juice and mustard in a small bowl. Mix until smooth and creamy. Heat 2 tbps of olive oil in a skillet over medium heat, add the prawns, season with salt, and chili pepper, and fry in the oil for 3 minutes on each side until prawns are pink. Set aside to a plate.
2. Place the arugula in a serving bowl and pour half of the dressing on the salad. Toss with 2 spoons until mixed, and add the remaining dressing. Divide salad into 4 plates and serve with prawns.

Nutrition Info:
- Per Servings 2g Carbs, 8g Protein, 20.3g Fat, 215 Calories

Chicken Stock And Green Bean Soup

Servings: 6
Cooking Time:1h 30 Mins

Ingredients:
- 2 tablespoons butter
- 1/2 onion, diced
- 2 ribs celery, diced
- 1 cup green beans
- 6 bacon slices
- What you'll need from the store cupboard:
- 3 cloves garlic, sliced
- 1 quart chicken stock

- 2 1/2 cups water
- 1 bay leaf
- Salt and ground black pepper to taste

Directions:

1. In a large pot over medium-low heat, melt the butter. Add the onions, celery, and sliced garlic, cook for 5-8 minutes, or until onions are soft.

2. Stir in in bacon slices, bay leaf, and green beans. Add chicken stock and water, stirring until well combined, and simmer for 1 hour and 15 minutes, or green beans are soft. Sprinkle with salt and black pepper before serving.

Nutrition Info:

- Per Servings 7g Carbs, 15.1g Protein, 11.3g Fat, 208.6 Calories

Coconut, Green Beans, And Shrimp Curry Soup

Servings: 4

Cooking Time: 20 Minutes

Ingredients:

- 2 tbsp ghee
- 1 lb jumbo shrimp, peeled and deveined
- 2 tsp ginger-garlic puree
- 2 tbsp red curry paste
- 6 oz coconut milk
- Salt and chili pepper to taste
- 1 bunch green beans, halved

Directions:

1. Melt ghee in a medium saucepan over medium heat. Add the shrimp, season with salt and pepper, and cook until they are opaque, 2 to 3 minutes. Remove shrimp to a plate. Add the ginger-garlic puree and red curry paste to the ghee and sauté for 2 minutes until fragrant.

2. Stir in the coconut milk; add the shrimp, salt, chili pepper, and green beans. Cook for 4 minutes. Reduce the heat to a simmer and cook an additional 3 minutes, occasionally stirring. Adjust taste with salt, fetch soup into serving bowls, and serve with cauli rice.

Nutrition Info:

- Per Servings 2g Carbs, 9g Protein, 35.4g Fat, 375 Calories

Brussels Sprouts Salad With Pecorino Romano

Servings: 6

Cooking Time: 35 Minutes

Ingredients:

- 2 lb Brussels sprouts, halved
- 3 tbsp olive oil
- Salt and black pepper to taste
- 2 ½ tbsp balsamic vinegar
- ¼ red cabbage, shredded
- 1 tbsp Dijon mustard
- 1 cup pecorino romano cheese, grated

Directions:

1. Preheat oven to 400ºF and line a baking sheet with foil. Toss the brussels sprouts with olive oil, a little salt, black pepper, and balsamic vinegar, in a bowl, and spread on the baking sheet in an even layer. Bake until tender on the inside and crispy on the outside, about 20 to 25 minutes.

2. Transfer to a salad bowl and add the red cabbage, Dijon mustard and half of the cheese. Mix until well combined. Sprinkle with the remaining cheese, share the salad onto serving plates, and serve with syrup-grilled salmon.

Nutrition Info:

- Per Servings 6g Carbs, 4g Protein, 18g Fat, 210 Calories

Chicken Taco Soup

Servings: 6

Cooking Time: 45 Minutes

Ingredients:

- 1-pound boneless chicken breast
- 1 tbsp taco seasoning
- 3 medium tomato chopped
- 1 medium onion chopped
- 2 Tablespoons garlic minced
- 5 cups water
- Salt and Pepper to taste
- Sour cream or tortilla chips for topping (optional)

Directions:

1. Add all ingredients in a heavy-bottomed pot except for garnish if using.

2. Bring to a boil, lower fire to a simmer, cover and cook for 30 minutes.

3. Remove chicken and shred. Return to the pot. Adjust seasoning with pepper and salt to taste.

4. Serve and enjoy with topping.

Nutrition Info:
- Per Servings 5.0g Carbs, 15.0g Protein, 2.0g Fat, 98 Calories

Slow Cooker Beer Soup With Cheddar & Sausage

Servings: 8
Cooking Time: 8 Hr

Ingredients:
- 1 cup heavy cream
- 10 ounces sausages, sliced
- 1 cup celery, chopped
- 1 cup carrots, chopped
- 4 garlic cloves, minced
- 8 ounces cream cheese
- 1 tsp red pepper flakes
- 6 ounces beer
- 16 ounces beef stock
- 1 onion, diced
- 1 cup cheddar cheese, grated
- Salt and black pepper, to taste
- Fresh cilantro, chopped, to garnish

Directions:
1. Turn on the slow cooker. Add beef stock, beer, sausages, carrots, onion, garlic, celery, salt, red pepper flakes, and black pepper, and stir to combine. Pour in enough water to cover all the ingredients by roughly 2 inches. Close the lid and cook for 6 hours on Low.
2. Open the lid and stir in the heavy cream, cheddar, and cream cheese, and cook for 2 more hours. Ladle the soup into bowls and garnish with cilantro before serving. Yummy!

Nutrition Info:
- Per Servings 4g Carbs, 5g Protein, 17g Fat, 244 Calories

Tomato Hamburger Soup

Servings: 8
Cooking Time: 25 Minutes

Ingredients:
- 1-pound ground beef
- 1 can V-8 juice
- 2 packages frozen vegetable mix
- 1 can condensed mushroom soup
- 2 teaspoon dried onion powder
- 5 tablespoons olive oil
- Salt and pepper to taste
- 1 cup water

Directions:
1. Place a pot over medium flame and heat for 2 minutes. Add oil and heat for a minute.
2. Sauté the beef until lightly browned, around 7 minutes. Season with salt, pepper, and onion powder.
3. Add the mushroom soup and water.
4. Give a good stir to combine everything.
5. Cover and bring to a boil, lower fire to a simmer and cook for 10 minutes.
6. Stir in vegetables. Cook until heated through around 5 minutes. Adjust seasoning if needed.
7. Serve and enjoy.

Nutrition Info:
- Per Servings 10g Carbs, 18.1g Protein, 14.8g Fat, 227 Calories

Strawberry, Mozzarella Salad

Servings: 3
Cooking Time: 10 Minutes

Ingredients:
- 5 ounces organic salad greens of your choice
- 2 medium cucumber, spiralized
- 2 cups strawberries, hulled and chopped
- 8 ounces mini mozzarella cheese balls
- ½ cup balsamic vinegar
- 5 tablespoons olive oil
- Salt to taste

Directions:
1. Toss all ingredients in a salad bowl.
2. Allow chilling in the fridge for at least 10 minutes before serving.

Nutrition Info:
- Per Servings 10g Carbs, 7g Protein, 31g Fat, 351 Calories

Vegan, Vegetable & Meatless Recipes

Vegan, Vegetable & Meatless Recipes

Chard Swiss Dip

Servings: 6
Cooking Time: 25 Minutes
Ingredients:
- 2 cups Swiss chard
- 1 cup tofu, pressed, drained, crumbled
- ½ cup almond milk
- 2 tsp nutritional yeast
- 2 garlic cloves, minced
- 2 tbsp olive oil
- Salt and pepper to taste
- ½ tsp paprika
- ½ tsp chopped fresh mint leaves

Directions:
1. Set oven to 400°F. Spray a nonstick cooking spray on a casserole pan. Boil Swiss chard until wilted. Using a blender, puree the remaining ingredients. Season with salt and pepper. Stir in the Swiss chard to get a homogeneous mixture. Bake for 13 minutes. Serve alongside baked vegetables.

Nutrition Info:
- Per Servings 7.9g Carbs, 2.9g Protein, 7.3g Fat, 105 Calories

Stir Fried Bok Choy

Servings: 4
Cooking Time: 15 Minutes
Ingredients:
- 4 cloves of garlic, minced
- 1 onion, chopped
- 2 heads bok choy, rinsed and chopped
- 2 tablespoons sesame oil
- 2 tablespoons sesame seeds, toasted
- 3 tablespoons oil
- Salt and pepper to taste

Directions:
1. Heat the oil in a pot for 2 minutes.
2. Sauté the garlic and onions until fragrant, around 3 minutes.
3. Stir in the bok choy, salt, and pepper.
4. Cover pan and cook for 5 minutes.
5. Stir and continue cooking for another 3 minutes.
6. Drizzle with sesame oil and sesame seeds on top

before serving.
Nutrition Info:
- Per Servings 5.2g Carbs, 21.5g Protein, 28.4g Fat, 358 Calories

Walnuts With Tofu

Servings: 4
Cooking Time: 13 Minutes
Ingredients:
- 3 tsp olive oil
- 1 cup extra firm tofu, cubed
- ¼ cup walnuts, chopped
- 1 ½ tbsp coconut aminos
- 3 tbsp vegetable broth
- ½ tsp smashed garlic
- 1 tsp cayenne pepper
- ½ tsp turmeric powder
- Sea salt and black pepper, to taste
- 2 tsp sunflower seeds

Directions:
1. Set a frying pan over medium heat. Warm the oil. Add in tofu and fry as you stir until they brown. Pour in the walnuts; turn temperature to higher and cook for 2 minutes. Stir in the remaining ingredients, set heat to medium-low and cook for 5 more minutes. Drizzle with hot sauce and serve!

Nutrition Info:
- Per Servings 5.3g Carbs, 8.3g Protein, 21.6g Fat, 232 Calories

Tomato Stuffed Avocado

Servings: 4
Cooking Time: 10 Minutes
Ingredients:
- 2 avocados, peeled and pitted
- 1 tomato, chopped
- ¼ cup walnuts, ground
- 2 carrots, chopped
- 1 garlic clove
- 1 tsp lemon juice
- 1 tbsp soy sauce
- Salt and black pepper, to taste

Directions:
1. Using a mixing bowl, mix soy sauce, carrots, avo-

cado pulp, lemon juice, walnuts, and garlic.

2. Add pepper and salt. Plate the mixture into the avocado halves. Scatter walnuts over to serve.

Nutrition Info:

• Per Servings 5.5g Carbs, 3.5g Protein, 24.8g Fat, 263 Calories

Zucchini Garlic Fries

Servings: 6

Cooking Time: 25 Minutes

Ingredients:

• ¼ teaspoon garlic powder
• ½ cup almond flour
• 2 large egg, beaten
• 3 medium zucchinis, sliced into fry sticks
• 3 tablespoons olive oil
• Salt and pepper to taste

Directions:

1. Preheat oven to 400oF.
2. Mix all ingredients in a bowl until the zucchini fries are well coated.
3. Place fries on a cookie sheet and spread evenly.
4. Put in the oven and cook for 15 minutes.
5. Stir fries, continue baking for an additional 10 minutes.

Nutrition Info:

• Per Servings 0.5g Carbs, 2g Protein, 8g Fat, 80 Calories

Cauliflower Fritters

Servings: 6

Cooking Time: 15 Minutes

Ingredients:

• 1 large cauliflower head, cut into florets
• 2 eggs, beaten
• ½ teaspoon turmeric
• 1 large onion, peeled and chopped
• ½ teaspoon salt
• ¼ teaspoon black pepper
• 6 tablespoons oil

Directions:

1. Place the cauliflower florets in a pot with water.
2. Bring to a boil and drain once cooked.
3. Place the cauliflower, eggs, onion, turmeric, salt, and pepper into the food processor.
4. Pulse until the mixture becomes coarse.
5. Transfer into a bowl. Using your hands, form six small flattened balls and place in the fridge for at least

1 hour until the mixture hardens.

6. Heat the oil in a skillet and fry the cauliflower patties for 3 minutes on each side.
7. Serve and enjoy.

Nutrition Info:

• Per Servings 2.28g Carbs, 3.9g Protein, 15.3g Fat, 157 Calories

Coconut Cauliflower & Parsnip Soup

Servings: 4

Cooking Time: 20 Minutes

Ingredients:

• 4 cups vegetable broth
• 2 heads cauliflower, cut into florets
• 1 cup parsnip, chopped
• 1 tbsp coconut oil
• 1 cup coconut milk
• ½ tsp red pepper flakes

Directions:

1. Add water in a pot set over medium-high heat and bring to a boil. Add in cauliflower florets and parsnip, cook for about 10 minutes. Add in broth and coconut oil. While on low heat, cook for an additional 5 minutes. Transfer the mixture to an immersion blender and puree.
2. Plate into four separate soup bowls; decorate each with red pepper flakes. Serve while warm.

Nutrition Info:

• Per Servings 7g Carbs, 2.7g Protein, 7.2g Fat, 94 Calories

Briam With Tomato Sauce

Servings: 4

Cooking Time: 70 Minutes

Ingredients:

• 3 tbsp olive oil
• 1 large eggplant, halved and sliced
• 1 large onion, thinly sliced
• 3 cloves garlic, sliced
• 5 tomatoes, diced
• 3 rutabagas, peeled and diced
• 1 cup sugar-free tomato sauce
• 4 zucchinis, sliced
• ¼ cup water
• Salt and black pepper to taste
• 1 tbsp dried oregano
• 2 tbsp chopped parsley

Directions:

1. Preheat the oven to 400°F. Heat the olive oil in a skillet over medium heat and cook the eggplants in it for 6 minutes to brown on the edges. After, remove to a medium bowl.

2. Sauté the onion and garlic in the oil for 3 minutes and add them to the eggplants. Turn the heat off.

3. In the eggplants bowl, mix in the tomatoes, rutabagas, tomato sauce, and zucchinis. Add the water and stir in the salt, pepper, oregano, and parsley. Pour the mixture in the casserole dish. Place the dish in the oven and bake for 45 to 60 minutes. Serve the briam warm on a bed of cauli rice.

Nutrition Info:
- Per Servings 12.5g Carbs, 11.3g Protein, 12g Fat, 365 Calories

Lemon Grilled Veggie

Servings: 4
Cooking Time: 20 Minutes

Ingredients:
- 2/3 eggplant
- 1 zucchini
- 10 oz. cheddar cheese
- 20 black olives
- 2 oz. leafy greens
- ½ cup olive oil
- 1 lemon, the juice
- 1 cup mayonnaise
- 4 tbsp almonds
- Salt and pepper

Directions:
1. Cut eggplant and zucchini lengthwise into half inch-thick slices. Season with salt to coat evenly. Set aside for 5-10 minutes.

2. Preheat the oven to 450 degrees F.

3. Pat zucchini and eggplant slices' surface dry with a kitchen towel.

4. Line a baking sheet with parchment paper and place slices on it. Spray with olive oil on top and season with pepper.

5. Bake for 15-20 minutes or until cooked through, flipping halfway.

6. Once done, transfer to a serving platter. Drizzle olive oil and lemon juice on top.

7. Serve with cheese cubes, almonds, olives, mayonnaise and leafy greens.

Nutrition Info:
- Per Servings 9g Carbs, 21g Protein, 99g Fat, 1013 Calories

Portobello Mushroom Burgers

Servings: 4
Cooking Time: 15 Minutes

Ingredients:
- 4 low carb buns
- 4 portobello mushroom caps
- 1 clove garlic, minced
- ½ tsp salt
- 2 tbsp olive oil
- ½ cup sliced roasted red peppers
- 2 medium tomatoes, chopped
- ¼ cup crumbled feta cheese
- 1 tbsp red wine vinegar
- 2 tbsp pitted kalamata olives, chopped
- ½ tsp dried oregano
- 2 cups baby salad greens

Directions:
1. Heat the grill pan over medium-high heat and while it heats, crush the garlic with salt in a bowl using the back of a spoon. Stir in 1 tablespoon of oil and brush the mushrooms and each inner side of the buns with the mixture.

2. Place the mushrooms in the heated pan and grill them on both sides for 8 minutes until tender.

3. Also, toast the buns in the pan until they are crisp, about 2 minutes. Set aside.

4. In a bowl, mix the red peppers, tomatoes, olives, feta cheese, vinegar, oregano, baby salad greens, and remaining oil; toss them. Assemble the burger: in a slice of bun, add a mushroom cap, a scoop of vegetables, and another slice of bread. Serve with cheese dip.

Nutrition Info:
- Per Servings 3g Carbs, 16g Protein, 8g Fat, 190 Calories

Vegetarian Burgers

Servings: 2
Cooking Time: 20 Minutes

Ingredients:
- 1 garlic cloves, minced
- 2 portobello mushrooms, sliced
- 1 tbsp coconut oil, melted
- 1 tbsp chopped basil
- 1 tbsp oregano
- 2 eggs, fried
- 2 low carb buns
- 2 tbsp mayonnaise
- 2 lettuce leaves

Directions:

1. Combine the melted coconut oil, garlic, herbs, and salt, in a bowl. Place the mushrooms in the bowl and coat well. Preheat the grill to medium heat. Grill the mushrooms for 2 minutes per side.

2. Cut the low carb buns in half. Add the lettuce leaves, grilled mushrooms, eggs, and mayonnaise. Top with the other bun half.

Nutrition Info:

• Per Servings 8.5g Carbs, 23g Protein, 55g Fat, 637 Calories

Keto Pizza Margherita

Servings: 2
Cooking Time: 40 Minutes

Ingredients:

• 6 ounces mozzarella
• 2 tbsp cream cheese
• 2 tbsp Parmesan cheese
• 1 tsp oregano
• ½ cup almond flour
• 2 tbsp psyllium husk
• Topping
• 4 ounces grated cheddar cheese
• ¼ cup Marinara sauce
• 1 bell pepper, sliced
• 1 tomato, sliced
• 2 tbsp chopped basil

Directions:

1. Preheat the oven to 400°F. Combine all crust ingredients in a large bowl, except the mozzarella.

2. Melt the mozzarella in a microwave. Stir it into the bowl. Mix with your hands to combine. Divide the dough in two. Roll out the two crusts in circles and place on a lined baking sheet. Bake for about 10 minutes. Top with the toppings. Return to the oven and bake for another 10 minutes.

Nutrition Info:

• Per Servings 3.7g Carbs, 31g Protein, 39g Fat, 510 Calories

Brussels Sprouts With Tofu

Servings: 4
Cooking Time: 20 Minutes

Ingredients:

• 2 tbsp olive oil
• 2 garlic cloves, minced
• ½ cup onion, chopped
• 10 ounces tofu, crumbled
• 2 tbsp water
• 2 tbsp soy sauce
• 1 tbsp tomato puree
• ½ pound Brussels sprouts, quartered
• Sea salt and black pepper, to taste

Directions:

1. Set a saucepan over medium-high heat and warm the oil. Add onion and garlic and cook until tender. Place in the soy sauce, water, and tofu. Cook for 5 minutes until the tofu starts to brown.

2. Add in brussels sprouts; apply pepper and salt for seasoning, reduce heat to low and cook for 13 minutes while stirring frequently. Serve while warm.

Nutrition Info:

• Per Servings 12.1g Carbs, 10.5g Protein, 11.7g Fat, 179 Calories

Cauliflower & Mushrooms Stuffed Peppers

Servings: 4
Cooking Time: 40 Minutes

Ingredients:

• 1 head cauliflower
• 4 bell peppers
• 1 cup mushrooms, sliced
• 1 ½ tbsp oil
• 1 onion, chopped
• 1 cup celery, chopped
• 1 garlic cloves, minced
• 1 tsp chili powder
• 2 tomatoes, pureed
• Sea salt and pepper, to taste

Directions:

1. To prepare cauliflower rice, grate the cauliflower into rice-size. Set in a kitchen towel to attract and remove any excess moisture. Set oven to 360°F.

2. Lightly oil a casserole dish. Chop off bell pepper tops, do away with the seeds and core. Line a baking pan with a parchment paper and roast the peppers for 18 minutes until the skin starts to brown.

3. Warm the oil over medium heat. Add in garlic, celery, and onion and sauté until soft and translucent. Stir in chili powder, mushrooms, and cauliflower rice. Cook for 6 minutes until the cauliflower rice becomes tender. Split the cauliflower mixture among the bell peppers. Set in the casserole dish. Combine pepper, salt, and tomatoes. Top the peppers with the tomato mixture. Bake for 10 minutes.

Nutrition Info:

- Per Servings 8.4g Carbs, 1.6g Protein, 4.8g Fat, 77 Calories

Curried Tofu

Servings: 6
Cooking Time: 15 Minutes

Ingredients:
- 2 cloves of garlic, minced
- 1 onion, cubed
- 12-ounce firm tofu, drained and cubed
- 1 teaspoon curry powder
- 1 tablespoon soy sauce
- ¼ teaspoon pepper
- 5 tablespoons olive oil

Directions:
1. Heat the oil in a skillet over medium flame.
2. Sauté the garlic and onion until fragrant.
3. Stir in the tofu and stir for 3 minutes.
4. Add the rest of the ingredients and adjust the water.
5. Close the lid and allow simmering for 10 minutes.
6. Serve and enjoy.

Nutrition Info:
- Per Servings 4.4g Carbs, 6.2g Protein, 14.1g Fat, 148 Calories

Garlic Lemon Mushrooms

Servings: 4
Cooking Time: 20 Minutes

Ingredients:
- 1/4 cup lemon juice
- 3 tablespoons minced fresh parsley
- 3 garlic cloves, minced
- 1-pound large fresh mushrooms
- 4 tablespoons olive oil
- Pepper to taste

Directions:
1. For the dressing, whisk together the first 5 ingredients. Toss mushrooms with 2 tablespoons dressing.
2. Grill mushrooms, covered, over medium-high heat until tender, 5-7 minutes per side. Toss with remaining dressing before serving.

Nutrition Info:
- Per Servings 6.8g Carbs, 4g Protein, 14g Fat, 160 Calories

Cauliflower Risotto With Mushrooms

Servings: 4
Cooking Time: 15 Minutes

Ingredients:
- 2 shallots, diced
- 3 tbsp olive oil
- ¼ cup veggie broth
- ⅓ cup Parmesan cheese
- 4 tbsp butter
- 3 tbsp chopped chives
- 2 pounds mushrooms, sliced
- 4 ½ cups riced cauliflower

Directions:
1. Heat 2 tbsp. oil in a saucepan. Add the mushrooms and cook over medium heat for about 3 minutes. Remove from the pan and set aside.
2. Heat the remaining oil and cook the shallots for 2 minutes. Stir in the cauliflower and broth, and cook until the liquid is absorbed. Stir in the rest of the ingredients.

Nutrition Info:
- Per Servings 8.4g Carbs, 11g Protein, 18g Fat, 264 Calories

Garlic 'n Sour Cream Zucchini Bake

Servings: 3
Cooking Time: 35 Minutes

Ingredients:
- 1 ½ cups zucchini slices
- 5 tablespoons olive oil
- 1 tablespoon minced garlic
- 1/4 cup grated Parmesan cheese
- 1 package cream cheese, softened
- Salt and pepper to taste

Directions:
1. Lightly grease a baking sheet with cooking spray.
2. Place zucchini in a bowl and put in oil oil and garlic.
3. Place zucchini slices in a single layer in.
4. Bake for 35 minutes at 390oF until crisp
5. In a bowl, whisk well, remaining ingreds.
6. Serve with zucchini

Nutrition Info:
- Per Servings 9.5g Carbs, 11.9g Prote 2.4g Fat, 385 Calories

Cremini Mushroom Stroganoff

Servings: 4
Cooking Time: 15 Minutes

Ingredients:
- 3 tbsp butter
- 1 white onion, chopped
- 4 cups cremini mushrooms, cubed
- 2 cups water
- ½ cup heavy cream
- ½ cup grated Parmesan cheese
- 1 ½ tbsp dried mixed herbs
- Salt and black pepper to taste

Directions:
1. Melt the butter in a saucepan over medium heat, sauté the onion for 3 minutes until soft.
2. Stir in the mushrooms and cook until tender, about 3 minutes. Add the water, mix, and bring to boil for 4 minutes until the water reduces slightly.
3. Pour in the heavy cream and parmesan cheese. Stir to melt the cheese. Also, mix in the dried herbs. Season with salt and pepper, simmer for 40 seconds and turn the heat off.
4. Ladle stroganoff over a bed of spaghetti squash and serve.

Nutrition Info:
- Per Servings 1g Carbs, 5g Protein, 28g Fat, 284 Calories

Egg And Tomato Salad

Servings: 2
Cooking Time: 1 Minute

Ingredients:
- 4 hardboiled eggs, peeled and sliced
- 2 tomatoes, chopped
- 1 small red onion, chopped
- 2 teaspoons lemon juice, freshly squeezed
- Salt pepper to taste
- 4 teaspoons olive oil

Directions:
1. Put all ingredients in a mixing bowl.
2. To coat all ingredients.
3. Garnish with parsley if desired.
4. Serve over toasted whole wheat bread.

Nutrition Info:
- Per Servings 9.1g Carbs, 14.7g Protein, 15.9g Fat, 189 Cals

Asparagus And Tarragon Flan

Servings: 4
Cooking Time: 65 Minutes

Ingredients:
- 16 asparagus, stems trimmed
- 1 cup water
- ½ cup whipping cream
- 1 cup almond milk
- 2 eggs + 2 egg yolks, beaten in a bowl
- 2 tbsp chopped tarragon, fresh
- Salt and black pepper to taste
- A small pinch of nutmeg
- 2 tbsp grated Parmesan cheese
- 3 cups water
- 2 tbsp butter, melted
- 1 tbsp butter, softened

Directions:
1. Pour the water and some salt in a pot, add the asparagus, and bring them to boil over medium heat on a stovetop for 6 minutes. Drain the asparagus; cut their tips and reserve for garnishing. Chop the remaining asparagus into small pieces.
2. In a blender, add the chopped asparagus, whipping cream, almond milk, tarragon, ½ teaspoon of salt, nutmeg, pepper, and Parmesan cheese. Process the ingredients on high speed until smooth. Pour the mixture through a sieve into a bowl and whisk the eggs into it.
3. Preheat the oven to 350°F. Grease the ramekins with softened butter and share the asparagus mixture among the ramekins. Pour the melted butter over each mixture and top with 2-3 asparagus tips. Pour the remaining water into a baking dish, place in the ramekins, and insert in the oven.
4. Bake for 45 minutes until their middle parts are no longer watery. Remove the ramekins and let cool. Garnish the flan with the asparagus tips and serve with chilled white wine.

Nutrition Info:
- Per Servings 2.5g Carbs, 12.5g Protein, 11.6g Fat, 264 Calories

Spicy Cauliflower Steaks With Steamed Green Beans

Servings: 4
Cooking Time: 20 Minutes

Ingredients:
- 2 heads cauliflower, sliced lengthwise into 'steaks'
- ¼ cup olive oil
- ¼ cup chili sauce
- 2 tsp erythritol
- Salt and black pepper to taste
- 2 shallots, diced
- 1 bunch green beans, trimmed
- 2 tbsp fresh lemon juice
- 1 cup water
- Dried parsley to garnish

Directions:
1. In a bowl, mix the olive oil, chili sauce, and erythritol. Brush the cauliflower with the mixture. Place them on the grill, close the lid, and grill for 6 minutes. Flip the cauliflower, cook further for 6 minutes.
2. Bring the water to boil over high heat, place the green beans in a sieve and set over the steam from the boiling water. Cover with a clean napkin to keep the steam trapped in the sieve. Cook for 6 minutes. After, remove to a bowl and toss with lemon juice.
3. Remove the grilled caulis to a plate; sprinkle with salt, pepper, shallots, and parsley. Serve with the steamed green beans.

Nutrition Info:
- Per Servings 4g Carbs, 2g Protein, 9g Fat, 118 Calories

Zucchini Lasagna With Ricotta And Spinach

Servings: 4
Cooking Time: 50 Minutes

Ingredients:
- Cooking spray
- 2 zucchinis, sliced
- Salt and black pepper to taste
- 2 cups ricotta cheese
- 2 cups shredded mozzarella cheese
- 3 cups tomato sauce
- 1 cup packed baby spinach

Directions:
1. Preheat oven to 370ºF and grease a baking dish with cooking spray.
2. Put the zucchini slices in a colander and sprinkle with salt. Let sit and drain liquid for 5 minutes and pat dry with paper towels. Mix the ricotta, mozzarella, salt, and pepper to evenly combine and spread ¼ cup of the mixture in the bottom of the baking dish.
3. Layer ⅓ of the zucchini slices on top spread 1 cup of tomato sauce over, and scatter a ⅓ cup of spinach on top. Repeat the layering process two more times to exhaust the ingredients while making sure to layer with the last ¼ cup of cheese mixture finally.
4. Grease one end of foil with cooking spray and cover the baking dish with the foil. Bake for 35 minutes, remove foil, and bake further for 5 to 10 minutes or until the cheese has a nice golden brown color. Remove the dish, sit for 5 minutes, make slices of the lasagna, and serve warm.

Nutrition Info:
- Per Servings 2g Carbs, 7g Protein, 39g Fat, 390 Calories

Classic Tangy Ratatouille

Servings: 6
Cooking Time: 47 Minutes

Ingredients:
- 2 eggplants, chopped
- 3 zucchinis, chopped
- 2 red onions, diced
- 1 can tomatoes
- 2 red bell peppers, cut in chunks
- 1 yellow bell pepper, cut in chunks
- 3 cloves garlic, sliced
- ½ cup basil leaves, chop half
- 4 sprigs thyme
- 1 tbsp balsamic vinegar
- 2 tbsp olive oil
- ½ lemon, zested

Directions:
1. In a casserole pot, heat the olive oil and sauté the eggplants, zucchinis, and bell peppers over medium heat for 5 minutes. Spoon the veggies into a large bowl.
2. In the same pan, sauté garlic, onions, and thyme leaves for 5 minutes and return the cooked veggies to the pan along with the canned tomatoes, balsamic vinegar, chopped basil, salt, and pepper to taste. Stir and cover the pot, and cook the ingredients on low heat for 30 minutes.
3. Open the lid and stir in the remaining basil leaves, lemon zest, and adjust the seasoning. Turn the heat off. Plate the ratatouille and serve with some low carb

crusted bread.

Nutrition Info:
• Per Servings 5.6g Carbs, 1.7g Protein, 12.1g Fat, 154 Calories

Sautéed Celeriac With Tomato Sauce

Servings: 4
Cooking Time: 20 Minutes

Ingredients:
• 2 tbsp olive oil
• 1 garlic clove, crushed
• 1 celeriac, sliced
• ¼ cup vegetable stock
• Sea salt and black pepper, to taste
• For the Sauce
• 2 tomatoes, halved
• 2 tbsp olive oil
• ½ cup onions, chopped
• 2 cloves garlic, minced
• 1 chili, minced
• 1 bunch fresh basil, chopped
• 1 tbsp fresh cilantro, chopped
• Salt and black pepper, to taste

Directions:
1. Set a pan over medium-high heat and warm olive oil. Add in garlic and sauté for 1 minute. Stir in celeriac slices, stock and cook until softened. Sprinkle with black pepper and salt; kill the heat. Brush olive oil to the tomato halves. Microwave for 15 minutes; get rid of any excess liquid.
2. Remove the cooked tomatoes to a food processor; add the rest of the ingredients for the sauce and puree to obtain the desired consistency. Serve the celeriac topped with tomato sauce.

Nutrition Info:
• Per Servings 3g Carbs, 0.9g Protein, 13.6g Fat, 135 Calories

Coconut Cauliflower Rice

Servings: 3
Cooking Time: 15 Minutes

Ingredients:
• 1 head cauliflower, grated
• ½ cup heavy cream
• ¼ cup butter, melted
• 3 cloves of garlic, minced
• 1 onion, chopped
• Salt and pepper to taste

Directions:

1. Place a nonstick saucepan on high fire and heat cream and butter.
2. Saute onion and garlic for 3 minutes.
3. Stir in grated cauliflower. Season with pepper and salt.
4. Cook until cauliflower is tender, around 5 minutes.
5. Turn off fire and let it set for 5 minutes.
6. Serve and enjoy.

Nutrition Info:
• Per Servings 9g Carbs, 3g Protein, 23g Fat, 246 Calories

Onion & Nuts Stuffed Mushrooms

Servings: 4
Cooking Time: 30 Minutes

Ingredients:
• 1 tbsp sesame oil
• 1 onion, chopped
• 1 garlic clove, minced
• 1 pound mushrooms, stems removed
• Salt and black pepper, to taste
• ¼ cup raw pine nuts
• 2 tbsp parsley, chopped

Directions:
1. Set oven to 360°F. Use a nonstick cooking spray to grease a large baking sheet. Into a frying pan, add sesame oil and warm. Place in garlic and onion and cook until soft.
2. Chop the mushroom stems and cook until tender. Turn off the heat, sprinkle with pepper and salt; add in pine nuts. Take the nut/mushroom mixture and stuff them to the mushroom caps and set on the baking sheet.
3. Bake the stuffed mushrooms for 30 minutes and remove to a wire rack to cool slightly. Add fresh parsley for garnish and serve.

Nutrition Info:
• Per Servings 7.4g Carbs, 4.8g Protein, 11.2g Fat, 139 Calories

Zoodles With Avocado & Olives

Servings: 4
Cooking Time: 15 Minutes

Ingredients:
• 4 zucchinis, julienned or spiralized
• ½ cup pesto
• 2 avocados, sliced
• 1 cup kalamata olives, chopped
• ¼ cup chopped basil

- 2 tbsp olive oil
- ¼ cup chopped sun-dried tomatoes

Directions:

1. Heat half of the olive oil in a pan over medium heat. Add zoodles and cook for 4 minutes. Transfer to a plate. Stir in pesto, basil, salt, tomatoes, and olives. Top with avocado slices.

Nutrition Info:

- Per Servings 8.4g Carbs, 6.3g Protein, 42g Fat, 449 Calories

Roasted Asparagus With Spicy Eggplant Dip

Servings: 6
Cooking Time: 35 Minutes

Ingredients:

- 1 ½ pounds asparagus spears, trimmed
- ¼ cup olive oil
- 1 tsp sea salt
- ½ tsp black pepper, to taste
- ½ tsp paprika
- For Eggplant Dip
- ¾ pound eggplants
- 2 tsp olive oil
- ½ cup scallions, chopped
- 2 cloves garlic, minced
- 1 tbsp fresh lemon juice
- ½ tsp chili pepper
- Salt and black pepper, to taste
- ¼ cup fresh cilantro, chopped

Directions:

1. Set the oven to 390°F. Line a parchment paper to a baking sheet. Add asparagus spears to the baking sheet. Toss with oil, paprika, pepper, and salt. Bake until cooked through for 9 minutes.
2. Set the oven to 425 °F. Add eggplants on a lined cookie sheet. Place under the broiler for about 20 minutes; let the eggplants to cool. Peel them and discard the stems. Place a frying pan over medium-high heat and warm olive oil. Add in garlic and onion and sauté until tender.
3. Using a food processor, pulse together black pepper, roasted eggplants, salt, lemon juice, scallion mixture, and chili pepper to mix evenly. Add cilantro for garnishing. Serve alongside roasted asparagus spears.

Nutrition Info:

- Per Servings 9g Carbs, 3.6g Protein, 12.1g Fat, 149 Calories

Garlic And Greens

Servings: 4
Cooking Time: 20 Minutes

Ingredients:

- 1-pound kale, trimmed and torn
- 1/4 cup chopped oil-packed sun-dried tomatoes
- 5 garlic cloves, minced
- 2 tablespoons minced fresh parsley
- 1/4 teaspoon salt
- 3 tablespoons olive oil

Directions:

1. In a 6-qt. stockpot, bring 1 inch. of water to a boil. Add kale; cook, covered, 10-15 minutes or until tender. Remove with a slotted spoon; discard cooking liquid.
2. In the same pot, heat oil over medium heat. Add tomatoes and garlic; cook and stir 1 minute. Add kale, parsley and salt; heat through, stirring occasionally.

Nutrition Info:

- Per Servings 9g Carbs, 6g Protein, 13g Fat, 160 Calories

Sausage Roll

Servings: 6
Cooking Time: 1 Hour And 15 Minutes

Ingredients:

- 6 vegan sausages (defrosted)
- 1 cup mushrooms
- 1 onion
- 2 fresh sage leaves
- 1 package tofu skin sheet
- Salt and pepper to taste
- 5 tablespoons olive oil

Directions:

1. Preheat the oven to 180°F/356°F assisted.
2. Defrost the vegan sausages.
3. Roughly chop the mushrooms and add them to a food processor. Process until mostly broken down. Peel and roughly chop the onions, then add them to the processor along with the defrosted vegan sausages, sage leaves, and a pinch of salt and pepper. Pour in the oil. Process until all the ingredients have mostly broken down, and only a few larger pieces remain.
4. Heat a frying pan on a medium heat. Once hot, transfer the mushroom mixture to the pan and fry for 20 minutes or until almost all of the moisture has evaporated, frequently stirring to prevent the mixture sticking to the pan.
5. Remove the mushroom mixture from the heat and

transfer to a plate. Leave to cool completely. Tip: if it's cold outside, we leave the mushroom mixture outdoors, so it cools quicker.

6. Meanwhile, either line a large baking tray with baking paper or (if the pastry already comes wrapped in a sheet of baking paper) roll out the tofu skin onto the tray and cut it in half both lengthways and widthways to create 4 equal-sized pieces of tofu skin.

7. Spoon a quarter of the mushroom mixture along the length of each rectangle of tofu skin and shape the mixture into a log. Add one vegan sausage and roll into a log.

8. Seal the roll by securing the edged with a toothpick.

9. Brush the sausage rolls with olive oil and bake for 40-45 minutes until golden brown. Enjoy!

Nutrition Info:
• Per Servings 3g Carbs, 0.9g Protein, 11g Fat, 113 Calories

Vegetable Tempeh Kabobs

Servings: 4
Cooking Time: 2 Hours 26 Minutes

Ingredients:
• 10 oz tempeh, cut into chunks
• 1 ½ cups water
• 1 red onion, cut into chunks
• 1 red bell pepper, cut chunks
• 1 yellow bell pepper, cut into chunks
• 2 tbsp olive oil
• 1 cup sugar-free barbecue sauce

Directions:
1. Bring the water to boil in a pot over medium heat and once it has boiled, turn the heat off, and add the tempeh. Cover the pot and let the tempeh steam for 5 minutes to remove its bitterness.

2. Drain the tempeh after. Pour the barbecue sauce in a bowl, add the tempeh to it, and coat with the sauce. Cover the bowl and marinate in the fridge for 2 hours.

3. Preheat a grill to 350ºF, and thread the tempeh, yellow bell pepper, red bell pepper, and onion.

4. Brush the grate of the grill with olive oil, place the skewers on it, and brush with barbecue sauce. Cook the kabobs for 3 minutes on each side while rotating and brushing with more barbecue sauce.

5. Once ready, transfer the kabobs to a plate and serve with lemon cauli couscous and a tomato sauce.

Nutrition Info:
• Per Servings 3.6g Carbs, 13.2g Protein, 15g Fat, 228 Calories

Tofu Sesame Skewers With Warm Kale Salad

Servings: 4
Cooking Time: 2 Hours 40 Minutes

Ingredients:
• 14 oz Firm tofu
• 4 tsp sesame oil
• 1 lemon, juiced
• 5 tbsp sugar-free soy sauce
• 3 tsp garlic powder
• 4 tbsp coconut flour
• ½ cup sesame seeds
• Warm Kale Salad:
• 4 cups chopped kale
• 2 tsp + 2 tsp olive oil
• 1 white onion, thinly sliced
• 3 cloves garlic, minced
• 1 cup sliced white mushrooms
• 1 tsp chopped rosemary
• Salt and black pepper to season
• 1 tbsp balsamic vinegar

Directions:
1. In a bowl, mix sesame oil, lemon juice, soy sauce, garlic powder, and coconut flour. Wrap the tofu in a paper towel, squeeze out as much liquid from it, and cut it into strips. Stick on the skewers, height wise. Place onto a plate, pour the soy sauce mixture over, and turn in the sauce to be adequately coated. Cover the dish with cling film and marinate in the fridge for 2 hours.

2. Heat the griddle pan over high heat. Pour the sesame seeds in a plate and roll the tofu skewers in the seeds for a generous coat. Grill the tofu in the griddle pan to be golden brown on both sides, about 12 minutes in total.

3. Heat 2 tablespoons of olive oil in a skillet over medium heat and sauté onion to begin browning for 10 minutes with continuous stirring. Add the remaining olive oil and mushrooms. Continue cooking for 10 minutes. Add garlic, rosemary, salt, pepper, and balsamic vinegar. Cook for 1 minute.

4. Put the kale in a salad bowl; when the onion mixture is ready, pour it on the kale and toss well. Serve the tofu skewers with the warm kale salad and a peanut butter dipping sauce.

Nutrition Info:
• Per Servings 6.1g Carbs, 5.6g Protein, 12.9g Fat, 263 Calories

Mushroom & Cauliflower Bake

Servings: 4
Cooking Time: 30 Minutes
Ingredients:
- Cooking spray
- 1 head cauliflower, cut into florets
- 8 ounces mushrooms, halved
- 2 garlic cloves, smashed
- 2 tomatoes, pureed
- ¼ cup coconut oil, melted
- 1 tsp chili paprika paste
- ¼ tsp marjoram
- ½ tsp curry powder
- Salt and black pepper, to taste

Directions:
1. Set oven to 390ºF. Apply a cooking spray to a baking dish. Lay mushrooms and cauliflower in the baking dish. Around the vegetables, scatter smashed garlic. Place in the pureed tomatoes. Sprinkle over melted coconut oil and place in chili paprika paste, curry, black pepper, salt, and marjoram. Roast for 25 minutes, turning once. Place in a serving plate and serve with green salad.

Nutrition Info:
- Per Servings 11.6g Carbs, 5g Protein, 6.7g Fat, 113 Calories

Crispy-topped Baked Vegetables

Servings: 4
Cooking Time: 40 Minutes
Ingredients:
- 2 tbsp olive oil
- 1 onion, chopped
- 1 celery, chopped
- 2 carrots, grated
- ½ pound turnip, sliced
- 1 cup vegetable broth
- 1 tsp turmeric
- Sea salt and black pepper, to taste
- ½ tsp liquid smoke
- 1 cup Parmesan cheese, shredded
- 2 tbsp fresh chives, chopped

Directions:
1. Set oven to 360ºF. Grease a baking dish with olive oil. Set a skillet over medium-high heat and warm olive oil. Sweat the onion until soft. Place in the turnip slices and celery. Cook for 4 minutes.
2. Remove the vegetable mixture to the baking dish.

Combine vegetable broth with turmeric, black pepper, liquid smoke, and salt.
3. Spread this mixture over the vegetables. Apply a topping of vegan parmesan cheese and bake for about 30 minutes. Decorate with fresh chives and serve.

Nutrition Info:
- Per Servings 8.6g Carbs, 16.3g Protein, 16.3g Fat, 242 Calories

Cheesy Cauliflower Falafel

Servings: 4
Cooking Time: 15 Minutes
Ingredients:
- 1 head cauliflower, cut into florets
- ⅓ cup silvered ground almonds
- ½ tsp mixed spice
- Salt and chili pepper to taste
- 3 tbsp coconut flour
- 3 fresh eggs
- 4 tbsp ghee

Directions:
1. Blend the cauli florets in a food processor until a grain meal consistency is formed. Pour the puree in a bowl, add the ground almonds, mixed spice, salt, chili pepper, and coconut flour, and mix until evenly combined.
2. Beat the eggs in a bowl until creamy in color and mix with the cauli mixture. Shape ¼ cup each into patties and set aside.
3. Melt ghee in a frying pan over medium heat and fry the patties for 5 minutes on each side to be firm and browned. Remove onto a wire rack to cool, share into serving plates, and top with tahini sauce.

Nutrition Info:
- Per Servings 2g Carbs, 8g Protein, 26g Fat, 315 Calories

Butternut Squash And Cauliflower Stew

Servings: 4
Cooking Time:10 Minutes
Ingredients:
- 3 cloves of garlic, minced
- 1 cup cauliflower florets
- 1 ½ cups butternut squash, cubed
- 2 ½ cups heavy cream
- Pepper and salt to taste
- 3 tbsp coconut oil

Directions:

1. Heat the oil in a pan and saute the garlic until fragrant.
2. Stir in the rest of the ingredients and season with salt and pepper to taste.
3. Close the lid and bring to a boil for 10 minutes.
4. Serve and enjoy.

Nutrition Info:
• Per Servings 10g Carbs, 2g Protein, 38.1g Fat, 385 Calories

Easy Vanilla Granola

Servings: 6
Cooking Time: 1 Hour

Ingredients:
• ½ cup hazelnuts, chopped
• 1 cup walnuts, chopped
• ⅓ cup flax meal
• ⅓ cup coconut milk
• ⅓ cup poppy seeds
• ⅓ cup pumpkin seeds
• 8 drops stevia
• ⅓ cup coconut oil, melted
• 1 ½ tsp vanilla paste
• 1 tsp ground cloves
• 1 tsp grated nutmeg
• 1 tsp lemon zest
• ⅓ cup water

Directions:
1. Set oven to 300ºF. Line a parchment paper to a baking sheet. Combine all ingredients. Spread the mixture onto the baking sheet in an even layer. Bake for 55 minutes, as you stir at intervals of 15 minutes. Let cool at room temperature.

Nutrition Info:
• Per Servings 5.1g Carbs, 9.3g Protein, 44.9g Fat, 449 Calories

Parmesan Roasted Cabbage

Servings: 4
Cooking Time: 25 Minutes

Ingredients:
• Cooking spray
• 1 large head green cabbage
• 4 tbsp melted butter
• 1 tsp garlic powder
• Salt and black pepper to taste
• 1 cup grated Parmesan cheese
• Grated Parmesan cheese for topping
• 1 tbsp chopped parsley to garnish

Directions:
1. Preheat oven to 400ºF, line a baking sheet with foil, and grease with cooking spray.
2. Stand the cabbage and run a knife from the top to bottom to cut the cabbage into wedges. Remove stems and wilted leaves. Mix the butter, garlic, salt, and black pepper until evenly combined.
3. Brush the mixture on all sides of the cabbage wedges and sprinkle with parmesan cheese.
4. Place on the baking sheet, and bake for 20 minutes to soften the cabbage and melt the cheese. Remove the cabbages when golden brown, plate and sprinkle with extra cheese and parsley. Serve warm with pan-glazed tofu.

Nutrition Info:
• Per Servings 4g Carbs, 17.5g Protein, 19.3g Fat, 268 Calories

Fish And Seafood Recipes

Fish And Seafood Recipes

Parmesan Fish Bake

Servings: 4
Cooking Time: 40 Minutes

Ingredients:
- Cooking spray
- 2 salmon fillets, cubed
- 3 white fish, cubed
- 1 broccoli, cut into florets
- 1 tbsp butter, melted
- Pink salt and black pepper to taste
- 1 cup crème fraiche
- ¼ cup grated Parmesan cheese
- Grated Parmesan cheese for topping

Directions:
1. Preheat oven to 400ºF and grease an 8 x 8 inches casserole dish with cooking spray. Toss the fish cubes and broccoli in butter and season with salt and pepper to taste. Spread in the greased dish.
2. Mix the crème fraiche with Parmesan cheese, pour and smear the cream on the fish, and sprinkle with some more Parmesan. Bake for 25 to 30 minutes until golden brown on top, take the dish out, sit for 5 minutes and spoon into plates. Serve with lemon-mustard asparagus.

Nutrition Info:
- Per Servings 4g Carbs, 28g Protein, 17g Fat, 354 Calories

Shrimp Stuffed Zucchini

Servings: 4
Cooking Time: 56 Minutes

Ingredients:
- 4 medium zucchinis
- 1 lb small shrimp, peeled, deveined
- 1 tbsp minced onion
- 2 tsp butter
- ¼ cup chopped tomatoes
- Salt and black pepper to taste
- 1 cup pork rinds, crushed
- 1 tbsp chopped basil leaves
- 2 tbsp melted butter

Directions:
1. Preheat the oven to 350ºF and trim off the top and bottom ends of the zucchinis. Lay them flat on a chopping board, and cut a ¼ -inch off the top to create a boat for the stuffing. Scoop out the seeds with a spoon and set the zucchinis aside.
2. Melt the firm butter in a small skillet and sauté the onion and tomato for 6 minutes. Transfer the mixture to a bowl and add the shrimp, half of the pork rinds, basil leaves, salt, and pepper.
3. Combine the ingredients and stuff the zucchini boats with the mixture. Sprinkle the top of the boats with the remaining pork rinds and drizzle the melted butter over them.
4. Place them on a baking sheet and bake them for 15 to 20 minutes. The shrimp should no longer be pink by this time. Remove the zucchinis after and serve with a tomato and mozzarella salad.

Nutrition Info:
- Per Servings 3.2g Carbs, 24.6g Protein, 14.4g Fat, 135 Calories

Simple Steamed Salmon Fillets

Servings: 3
Cooking Time: 15 Minutes

Ingredients:
- 10 oz. salmon fillets
- 2 tbsp. coconut aminos
- 2 tbsp. lemon juice, freshly squeezed
- 1 tsp. sesame seeds, toasted
- 3 tbsp sesame oil
- Salt and pepper to taste

Directions:
1. Place a trivet in a large saucepan and pour a cup or two of water into the pan. Bring to a boil.
2. Place salmon in a heatproof dish that fits inside the saucepan. Season salmon with pepper and salt. Drizzle with coconut aminos, lemon juice, sesame oil, and sesame seeds.
3. Seal dish with foil. Place the dish on the trivet inside the saucepan. Cover and steam for 15 minutes.
4. Serve and enjoy.

Nutrition Info:
- Per Servings 2.6g Carbs, 20.1g Protein, 17.4g Fat, 210 Calories

Steamed Cod With Ginger

Servings: 4
Cooking Time: 15 Minutes
Ingredients:
- 4 cod fillets, skin removed
- 3 tbsp. lemon juice, freshly squeezed
- 2 tbsp. coconut aminos
- 2 tbsp. grated ginger
- 6 scallions, chopped
- 5 tbsp coconut oil
- Pepper and salt to taste

Directions:
1. Place a trivet in a large saucepan and pour a cup or two of water into the pan. Bring to a boil.
2. In a small bowl, whisk well lemon juice, coconut aminos, coconut oil, and grated ginger.
3. Place scallions in a heatproof dish that fits inside a saucepan. Season scallions mon with pepper and salt. Drizzle with ginger mixture. Sprinkle scallions on top.
4. Seal dish with foil. Place the dish on the trivet inside the saucepan. Cover and steam for 15 minutes.
5. Serve and enjoy.

Nutrition Info:
- Per Servings 10g Carbs, 28.3g Protein, 40g Fat, 514 Calories

Thyme-sesame Crusted Halibut

Servings: 2
Cooking Time: 15 Minutes
Ingredients:
- 8 oz. halibut, cut into 2 portions
- 1 tbsp. lemon juice, freshly squeezed
- 1 tsp. dried thyme leaves
- 1 tbsp. sesame seeds, toasted
- Salt and pepper to taste

Directions:
1. Place a trivet in a large saucepan and pour a cup or two of water into the pan. Bring it to a boil.
2. Place halibut in a heatproof dish that fits inside a saucepan. Season with lemon juice, salt, and pepper. Sprinkle with dried thyme leaves and sesame seeds.
3. Seal dish with foil. Place the dish on the trivet inside the saucepan. Cover and steam for 15 minutes.
4. Serve and enjoy.

Nutrition Info:
- Per Servings 4.2g Carbs, 17.5g Protein, 17.7g Fat, 246 Calories

Five-spice Steamed Tilapia

Servings: 4
Cooking Time: 15 Minutes
Ingredients:
- 1 lb. Tilapia fillets,
- 1 tsp. Chinese five-spice powder
- 3 tablespoons coconut oil
- 3 scallions, sliced thinly
- Salt and pepper to taste

Directions:
1. Place a trivet in a large saucepan and pour a cup of water into the pan. Bring to a boil.
2. Place tilapia in a heatproof dish that fits inside a saucepan. Drizzle oil on tilapia. Season with salt, pepper, and Chinese five-spice powder. Garnish with scallions.
3. Seal dish with foil. Place the dish on the trivet inside the saucepan. Cover and steam for 15 minutes.
4. Serve and enjoy.

Nutrition Info:
- Per Servings 0.9g Carbs, 24g Protein, 12.3g Fat, 201 Calories

Boiled Garlic Clams

Servings: 6
Cooking Time: 10 Minutes
Ingredients:
- 3 tbsp butter
- 6 cloves of garlic
- 50 small clams in the shell, scrubbed
- ½ cup fresh parsley, chopped
- 4 tbsp. extra virgin olive oil
- 1 cup water
- Salt and pepper to taste

Directions:
1. Heat the olive oil and butter in a large pot placed on medium-high fire for a minute.
2. Stir in the garlic and cook until fragrant and slightly browned.
3. Stir in the clams, water, and parsley. Season with salt and pepper to taste.
4. Cover and cook for 5 minutes or until clams have opened.
5. Discard unopened clams and serve.

Nutrition Info:
- Per Servings 0.9g Carbs, 11.3g Protein, 12.8g Fat, 159 Calories

Coconut Milk Sauce Over Crabs

Servings: 6
Cooking Time: 20 Minutes

Ingredients:
- 2-pounds crab quartered
- 1 can coconut milk
- 1 thumb-size ginger, sliced
- 1 onion, chopped
- 3 cloves of garlic, minced
- Pepper and salt to taste

Directions:
1. Place a heavy-bottomed pot on medium-high fire and add all ingredients.
2. Cover and bring to a boil, lower fire to a simmer, and simmer for 20 minutes.
3. Serve and enjoy.

Nutrition Info:
- Per Servings 6.3g Carbs, 29.3g Protein, 11.3g Fat, 244.1 Calories

Trout And Fennel Parcels

Servings: 4
Cooking Time: 20 Minutes

Ingredients:
- ½ lb deboned trout, butterflied
- Salt and black pepper to season
- 3 tbsp olive oil + extra for tossing
- 4 sprigs rosemary
- 4 sprigs thyme
- 4 butter cubes
- 1 cup thinly sliced fennel
- 1 medium red onion, sliced
- 8 lemon slices
- 3 tsp capers to garnish

Directions:
1. Preheat the oven to 400ºF. Cut out parchment paper wide enough for each trout. In a bowl, toss the fennel and onion with a little bit of olive oil and share into the middle parts of the papers.
2. Place the fish on each veggie mound, top with a drizzle of olive oil each, salt and pepper, a sprig of rosemary and thyme, and 1 cube of butter. Also, lay the lemon slices on the fish. Wrap and close the fish packets securely, and place them on a baking sheet.
3. Bake in the oven for 15 minutes, and remove once ready. Plate them and garnish the fish with capers and serve with a squash mash.

Nutrition Info:

- Per Servings 2.8g Carbs, 17g Protein, 9.3g Fat, 234 Calories

Rosemary-lemon Shrimps

Servings: 4
Cooking Time: 8 Minutes

Ingredients:
- 5 tablespoons butter
- ½ cup lemon juice, freshly squeezed
- 1 ½ lb. shrimps, peeled and deveined
- ¼ cup coconut aminos
- 1 tsp rosemary
- Pepper to taste

Directions:
1. Place all ingredients in a large pan on a high fire.
2. Boil for 8 minutes or until shrimps are pink.
3. Serve and enjoy.

Nutrition Info:
- Per Servings 3.7g Carbs, 35.8g Protein, 17.9g Fat, 315 Calories

Coconut Curry Cod

Servings: 4
Cooking Time: 17 Minutes

Ingredients:
- 4 cod fillets
- 1 ½ cups coconut milk, freshly squeezed if possible
- 2 tsp. grated ginger
- 2 tsp. curry powder
- 1 sprig cilantro, chopped
- Salt and pepper to taste

Directions:
1. Add all ingredients in a nonstick saucepan. Cover and cook for 10 minutes on a high fire.
2. Lower fire to a simmer and simmer for 7 minutes.
3. Season with pepper and salt.
4. Serve and enjoy.

Nutrition Info:
- Per Servings 5.7g Carbs, 19.7g Protein, 22.1g Fat, 291 Calories

Halibut En Papillote

Servings: 4

Cooking Time: 15 Minutes

Ingredients:

- 4 halibut fillets
- ½ tbsp. grated ginger
- 1 cup chopped tomatoes
- 1 shallot, thinly sliced
- 1 lemon
- 5 tbsp olive oil
- Salt and pepper to taste

Directions:

1. Slice lemon in half. Slice one lemon in circles.
2. Juice the other half of the lemon in a small bowl. Mix in grated ginger and season with pepper and salt.
3. Place a trivet in a large saucepan and pour a cup or two of water into the pan. Bring to a boil.
4. Get 4 large foil and place one fillet in the middle of each foil. Season with fillet salt and pepper. Drizzle with olive oil. Add the grated ginger, tomatoes, and shallots equally. Fold the foil to create a pouch and crimp the edges.
5. Place the foil containing the fish on the trivet. Cover saucepan and steam for 15 minutes.
6. Serve and enjoy in pouches.

Nutrition Info:

- Per Servings 2.7g Carbs, 20.3g Protein, 32.3g Fat, 410 Calories

Shrimp Spread

Servings: 20

Cooking Time: 0 Minutes

Ingredients:

- 1 package cream cheese, softened
- 1/2 cup sour cream
- 1 cup seafood cocktail sauce
- 12 ounces frozen cooked salad shrimp, thawed
- 1 medium green pepper, chopped
- Pepper

Directions:

1. In a large bowl, beat the cream cheese, and sour cream until smooth.
2. Spread mixture on a round 12-inch serving platter.
3. Top with seafood sauce.
4. Sprinkle with shrimp and green peppers. Cover and refrigerate.
5. Serve with crackers.

Nutrition Info:

- Per Servings 4g Carbs, 8g Protein, 10g Fat, 136 Calories

Halibut With Pesto

Servings: 4

Cooking Time: 15 Minutes

Ingredients:

- 4 halibut fillets
- 1 cup basil leaves
- 2 cloves of garlic, minced
- 1 tbsp. lemon juice, freshly squeezed
- 2 tbsp pine nuts
- 2 tbsp. oil, preferably extra virgin olive oil
- Salt and pepper to taste

Directions:

1. In a food processor, pulse the basil, olive oil, pine nuts, garlic, and lemon juice until coarse. Season with salt and pepper to taste.
2. Place a trivet in a large saucepan and pour a cup or two of water into the pan. Bring to a boil.
3. Place salmon in a heatproof dish that fits inside a saucepan. Season salmon with pepper and salt. Drizzle with pesto sauce.
4. Seal dish with foil. Place the dish on the trivet inside the saucepan. Cover and steam for 15 minutes.
5. Serve and enjoy.

Nutrition Info:

- Per Servings 0.8g Carbs, 75.8g Protein, 8.4g Fat, 401 Calories

Avocado Salad With Shrimp

Serves: 4

Cooking Time:10 Minutes

Ingredients:

- 2 tomatoes, sliced into cubes
- 2 medium avocados, cut into large pieces
- 3 tablespoons red onion, diced
- ½ large lettuce, chopped
- 2 lbs. shrimp, peeled and deveined
- For the Lime Vinaigrette Dressing
- 2 cloves garlic, minced
- 1 ½ teaspoon Dijon mustard
- 1/3 cup extra virgin olive oil
- salt and pepper to taste
- 1/3 cup lime juice

Directions:

1. Add the peeled and deveined shrimp and 2 quarts of water to a cooking pot and print to a boil, lower the heat and let them simmer for 1-2 minutes until the

shrimp is pink. Set aside and let them cool.

2. Next add the chopped lettuce in a large bowl. Then add the avocado, tomatoes, shrimp and red onion.

3. In a small bowl whisk together the Dijon mustard, garlic, olive oil and lime juice. Mix well.

4. Pour the lime vinaigrette dressing over the salad and serve.

Nutrition Info:

• Per serving: 7g Carbs; 43.5g Protein; 17.6g Fat; 377 Calories;

Baked Codfish With Lemon

Serves: 4

Cooking Time:25 Minutes

Ingredients:

• 4 fillets codfish
• 1 teaspoon salt
• 1 teaspoon pepper
• 2 tablespoons olive oil
• 2 teaspoons dried basil
• 2 tablespoons melted butter
• 1 teaspoon dried thyme
• 1/3 teaspoon onion powder
• 2 lemons, juiced
• lemon wedges, for garnish

Directions:

1. Preheat the oven to 400°F.

2. In a medium bowl combine the lemon juice, onion powder, olive oil, dried basil and thyme. Stir well. Season the fillets with salt and pepper.

3. Top each fillet into the mixture. Then place the fillets into a medium baking dish, greased with melted butter.

4. Bake the codfish fillets for 15-20 minutes. Serve with fresh lemon wedges. Enjoy!

Nutrition Info:

• Per serving: 3.9g Carbs; 21.2g Protein; 23.6g Fat; 308 Calories

Sicilian-style Zoodle Spaghetti

Servings: 2

Cooking Time: 10 Minutes

Ingredients:

• 4 cups zoodles (spiralled zucchini)
• 2 ounces cubed bacon
• 4 ounces canned sardines, chopped
• ½ cup canned chopped tomatoes
• 1 tbsp capers
• 1 tbsp parsley

• 1 tsp minced garlic

Directions:

1. Pour some of the sardine oil in a pan. Add garlic and cook for 1 minute. Add the bacon and cook for 2 more minutes. Stir in the tomatoes and let simmer for 5 minutes. Add zoodles and sardines and cook for 3 minutes.

Nutrition Info:

• Per Servings 6g Carbs, 20g Protein, 31g Fat, 355 Calories

Cedar Salmon With Green Onion

Servings: 5

Cooking Time: 20 Mins

Ingredients:

• 3 untreated cedar planks
• 1/4 cup. chopped green onions
• 1 tablespoon. grated fresh ginger root
• 1 teaspoon. minced garlic
• 2 salmon fillets, skin removed
• 1/3 cup. olive oil
• 1/3 cup. mayo
• 1 1/2 tablespoons. rice vinegar

Directions:

1. Soak cedar planks in warm water for 1 hour more.

2. Whisk olive oil, rice vinegar, mayo, green onions, ginger, and garlic in a bowl. Marinade salmon fillets to coat completely. Cover the bowl with plastic wrap and marinate for 15 to 60 minutes.

3. Preheat an outdoor grill over medium heat. Lay planks on the center of hot grate Place the salmon fillets onto the planks and remove the marinade. Cover the grill and cook until cooked through, about 20 minutes, or until salmon is done to your liking. Serve the salmon on a platter right off the planks.

Nutrition Info:

• Per Servings 10g Carbs, 18g Protein, 27g Fat, 355 Calories

Lemon-rosemary Shrimps

Servings: 4

Cooking Time: 12 Minutes

Ingredients:

• ½ cup lemon juice, freshly squeezed
• 1 ½ lb. shrimps, peeled and deveined
• 2 tbsp fresh rosemary
• ¼ cup coconut aminos
• 2 tbsp butter

- Pepper to taste
- 4 tbsp olive oil

Directions:

1. Place a nonstick saucepan on medium-high fire and heat oil and butter for 2 minutes.
2. Stir in shrimps and coconut aminos. Season with pepper. Sauté for 5 minutes.
3. Add remaining ingredients and cook for another 5 minutes while stirring frequently.
4. Serve and enjoy.

Nutrition Info:

- Per Servings 3.7g Carbs, 35.8g Protein, 22.4g Fat, 359 Calories

Baked Salmon With Pistachio Crust

Serves:4

Cooking Time:35 Minutes

Ingredients:

- 4 salmon fillets
- ¼ cup mayonnaise
- ½ cup ground pistachios
- 1 chopped shallot
- 2 tsp lemon zest
- 1 tbsp olive oil
- A pinch of pepper
- 1 cup heavy cream

Directions:

1. Preheat oven to 375 °F. Brush salmon with mayo and season with salt and pepper. Coat with pistachios. Place in a lined baking dish and bake for 15 minutes. Heat the olive oil in a saucepan and sauté shallot for 3 minutes. Stir in heavy cream and lemon zest. Bring to a boil and cook until thickened. Serve salmon with the sauce.

Nutrition Info:

- Per Serves 6g Carbs; 34g Protein; 47g Fat ; 563 Calories

Angel Hair Shirataki With Creamy Shrimp

Serves:4

Cooking Time 25 Minutes

Ingredients:

- 2 (8 oz) packs angel hair shirataki noodles
- 1 tbsp olive oil
- 1 lb shrimp, deveined
- 2 tbsp unsalted butter
- 6 garlic cloves, minced

- ½ cup dry white wine
- 1 ½ cups heavy cream
- ½ cup grated Asiago cheese
- 2 tbsp chopped fresh parsley

Directions:

1. Heat olive oil in a skillet, season the shrimp with salt and pepper, and cook on both sides, 2 minutes; set aside. Melt butter in the skillet and sauté garlic. Stir in wine and cook until reduced by half, scraping the bottom of the pan to deglaze. Stir in heavy cream. Let simmer for 1 minute and stir in Asiago cheese to melt. Return the shrimp to the sauce and sprinkle the parsley on top. Bring 2 cups of water to a boi. Strain shirataki pasta and rinse under hot running water. Allow proper draining and pour the shirataki pasta into the boiling water. Cook for 3 minutes and strain again. Place a dry skillet and stir-fry the pasta until dry, 1-2 minutes. Season with salt and plate. Top with the shrimp sauce and serve.

Nutrition Info:

- Per Serves 6.3g Carbs; 33g Protein ; 32g Fats; 493 Calories

Asian-style Steamed Mussels

Serves:6

Cooking Time:25 Minutes

Ingredients:

- 5 tbsp sesame oil
- 1 onion, chopped
- 3 lb mussels, cleaned
- 2 garlic cloves, minced
- 12 oz coconut milk
- 16 oz white wine
- 1 lime, juiced
- 2 tsp red curry powder
- 2 tbsp cilantro, chopped

Directions:

1. Warm the sesame oil in a saucepan over medium heat and cook onion and garlic cloves for 3 minutes. Pour in wine, coconut milk, and curry powder and cook for 5 minutes. Add mussels, turn off the heat, cover the saucepan, and steam the mussels until the shells open up, 5 minutes. Discard any closed mussels. Top with cilantro and serve.

Nutrition Info:

- Per Serves 5.4g Carbs ; 28.2g Protein;16g Fat ; 323 Calories

Avocado And Salmon

Serves: 2

Cooking Time: 0 Minutes

Ingredients:
- 1 avocado, halved, pitted
- 2 oz flaked salmon, packed in water
- 1 tbsp mayonnaise
- 1 tbsp grated cheddar cheese
- Seasoning:
- 1/8 tsp salt
- 2 tbsp coconut oil

Directions:

1. Prepare the avocado and for this, cut avocado in half and then remove its seed.Drain the salmon, add it in a bowl along with remaining ingredients, stir well and then scoop into the hollow on an avocado half. Serve.

Nutrition Info:
- 3 g Carbs; 19 g Protein; 48 g Fats; 525 Calories

Chipotle Salmon Asparagus

Servings: 2

Cooking Time: 15 Minutes

Ingredients:
- 1-lb salmon fillet, skin on
- 2 teaspoon chipotle paste
- A handful of asparagus spears, trimmed
- 1 lemon, sliced thinly
- A pinch of rosemary
- Salt to taste
- 5 tbsp olive oil

Directions:

1. In a heat-proof dish that fits inside the saucepan, add asparagus spears on the bottom of the dish. Place fish, top with rosemary, and lemon slices. Season with chipotle paste and salt. Drizzle with olive oil. Cover dish with foil.

2. Place a large saucepan on the medium-high fire. Place a trivet inside the saucepan and fill the pan half-way with water. Cover and bring to a boil.

3. Place dish on the trivet.

4. Cover pan and steam for 10 minutes. Let it rest in pan for another 5 minutes.

5. Serve and enjoy topped with pepper.

Nutrition Info:
- Per Servings 2.8g Carbs, 35.0g Protein, 50.7g Fat, 651 Calories

Lemon Chili Halibut

Servings: 2

Cooking Time: 15 Minutes

Ingredients:
- 1-lb halibut fillets
- 1 lemon, sliced
- 1 tablespoon chili pepper flakes
- Pepper and salt to taste
- 4 tbsp olive oil

Directions:

1. In a heat-proof dish that fits inside saucepan, place fish. Top fish with chili flakes, lemon slices, salt, and pepper. Drizzle with olive oil. Cover dish with foil

2. Place a large saucepan on the medium-high fire. Place a trivet inside the saucepan and fill the pan half-way with water. Cover and bring to a boil.

3. Place dish on the trivet.

4. Cover pan and steam for 10 minutes. Let it rest in pan for another 5 minutes.

5. Serve and enjoy topped with pepper.

Nutrition Info:
- Per Servings 4.2g Carbs, 42.7g Protein, 58.4g Fat, 675 Calories

Air Fryer Seasoned Salmon Fillets

Servings: 4

Cooking Time: 10 Mins

Ingredients:
- 2 lbs. salmon fillets
- 1 tsp. stevia
- 2 tbsp. whole grain mustard
- 1 clove of garlic, minced
- 1/2 tsp. thyme leaves
- 2 tsp. extra-virgin olive oil
- Cooking spray
- Salt and black pepper to taste

Directions:

1. Preheat your Air Fryer to 390 degrees F.

2. Season salmon fillets with salt and pepper.

3. Add together the mustard, garlic, stevia, thyme, and oil in a bowl, stir to combined well. Rub the seasoning mixture on top of salmon fillets.

4. Spray the Air Fryer basket with cooking spray and cook seasoned fillets for 10 minutes until crispy. Let it cool before serving.

Nutrition Info:
- Per Servings 14g Carbs, 18g Protein, 10g Fat, 238 Calories

Creamy Hoki With Almond Bread Crust

Servings: 4
Cooking Time: 50 Minutes
Ingredients:
- 1 cup flaked smoked hoki, bones removed
- 1 cup cubed hoki fillets, cubed
- 4 eggs
- 1 cup water
- 3 tbsp almond flour
- 1 medium white onion, sliced
- 2 cups sour cream
- 1 tbsp chopped parsley
- 1 cup pork rinds, crushed
- 1 cup grated cheddar cheese
- Salt and black pepper to taste
- Cooking spray

Directions:
1. Preheat the oven to 360ºF and lightly grease a baking dish with cooking spray.
2. Then, boil the eggs in water in a pot over medium heat to be well done for 12 minutes, run the eggs under cold water and peel the shells. After, place on a cutting board and chop them.
3. Melt the butter in a saucepan over medium heat and sauté the onion for about 4 minutes. Turn the heat off and stir the almond flour into it to form a roux. Turn the heat back on and cook the roux to be golden brown and stir in the cream until the mixture is smooth. Season with salt and pepper, and stir in the parsley.
4. Spread the smoked and cubed fish in the baking dish, sprinkle the eggs on top, and spoon the sauce over. In a bowl, mix the pork rinds with the cheddar cheese, and sprinkle it over the sauce.
5. Bake the casserole in the oven for 20 minutes until the top is golden and the sauce and cheese are bubbly. Remove the bake after and serve with a steamed green vegetable mix.

Nutrition Info:
- Per Servings 3.5g Carbs, 28.5g Protein, 27g Fat, 386 Calories

Steamed Ginger Scallion Fish

Servings:
Cooking Time: 15 Minutes
Ingredients:
- 3 tablespoons soy sauce, low sodium
- 2 tablespoons rice wine
- 1 teaspoon minced ginger
- 1 teaspoon garlic
- 1-pound firm white fish
- Pepper to taste
- 4 tbsps sesame oil

Directions:
1. In a heat-proof dish that fits inside the saucepan, add all ingredients. Mix well.
2. Place a large saucepan on the medium-high fire. Place a trivet inside the saucepan and fill the pan halfway with water. Cover and bring to a boil.
3. Cover dish with foil and place on a trivet.
4. Cover pan and steam for 10 minutes. Let it rest in pan for another 5 minutes.
5. Serve and enjoy.

Nutrition Info:
- Per Servings 5.5g Carbs, 44.9g Protein, 23.1g Fat, 409.5 Calories

Simply Steamed Alaskan Cod

Servings: 2
Cooking Time: 15 Minutes
Ingredients:
- 1-lb fillet wild Alaskan Cod
- 1 cup cherry tomatoes, halved
- 1 tbsp balsamic vinegar
- 1 tbsp fresh basil chopped
- Salt and pepper to taste
- 5 tbsp olive oil

Directions:
1. In a heat-proof dish that fits inside the saucepan, add all ingredients except for basil. Mix well.
2. Place a large saucepan on the medium-high fire. Place a trivet inside the saucepan and fill pan halfway with water. Cover and bring to a boil.
3. Cover dish with foil and place on a trivet.
4. Cover pan and steam for 10 minutes. Let it rest in pan for another 5 minutes.
5. Serve and enjoy topped with fresh basil.

Nutrition Info:
- Per Servings 4.2g Carbs, 41.0g Protein, 36.6g Fat, 495.2 Calories

Enchilada Sauce On Mahi Mahi

Servings: 2

Cooking Time: 15 Minutes

Ingredients:

- 2 Mahi fillets, fresh
- ¼ cup commercial enchilada sauce
- Pepper to taste

Directions:

1. In a heat-proof dish that fits inside saucepan, place fish and top with enchilada sauce.
2. Place a large saucepan on the medium-high fire. Place a trivet inside the saucepan and fill the pan halfway with water. Cover and bring to a boil.
3. Cover dish with foil and place on a trivet.
4. Cover pan and steam for 10 minutes. Let it rest in pan for another 5 minutes.
5. Serve and enjoy topped with pepper.

Nutrition Info:

- Per Servings 8.9g Carbs, 19.8g Protein, 15.9g Fat, 257 Calories

Steamed Chili-rubbed Tilapia

Servings: 4

Cooking Time: 15 Minutes

Ingredients:

- 1 lb. tilapia fillet, skin removed
- 2 tbsp. chili powder
- 3 cloves garlic, peeled and minced
- 2 tbsp. extra virgin olive oil
- 2 tbsp soy sauce

Directions:

1. Place a trivet in a large saucepan and pour a cup or two of water into the pan. Bring it to a boil.
2. Place tilapia in a heatproof dish that fits inside a saucepan. Drizzle soy sauce and oil on the filet. Season with chili powder and garlic.
3. Seal dish with foil. Place the dish on the trivet inside the saucepan. Cover and steam for 15 minutes.
4. Serve and enjoy.

Nutrition Info:

- Per Servings 2g Carbs, 26g Protein, 10g Fat, 211 Calories

Buttery Almond Lemon Tilapia

Servings: 4

Cooking Time: 10 Minutes

Ingredients:

- 4 tilapia fillets
- 1/4 cup butter, cubed
- 1/4 cup white wine or chicken broth
- 2 tablespoons lemon juice
- 1/4 cup sliced almonds
- 1/2 teaspoon salt
- 1/4 teaspoon pepper
- 1 tablespoon olive oil

Directions:

1. Sprinkle fillets with salt and pepper. In a large non-stick skillet, heat oil over medium heat.
2. Add fillets; cook until fish just begins to flake easily with a fork, 2-3 minutes on each side. Remove and keep warm.
3. Add butter, wine and lemon juice to the same pan; cook and stir until butter is melted.
4. Serve with fish; sprinkle with almonds.

Nutrition Info:

- Per Servings 2g Carbs, 22g Protein, 19g Fat, 269 Calories

Sautéed Savory Shrimps

Servings: 8

Cooking Time: 15 Minutes

Ingredients:

- 2 pounds shrimp, peeled and deveined
- 4 cloves garlic, minced
- ½ cup chicken stock, low sodium
- 1 tablespoon lemon juice
- Salt and pepper
- 5 tablespoons oil

Directions:

1. Place a heavy-bottomed pot on medium-high fire and heat pot for 3 minutes.
2. Once hot, add oil and stir around to coat pot with oil.
3. Sauté the garlic and corn for 5 minutes.
4. Add remaining ingredients and mix well.
5. Cover and bring to a boil, lower fire to a simmer, and simmer for 5 minutes.
6. Serve and enjoy.

Nutrition Info:

- Per Servings 1.7g Carbs, 25.2g Protein, 9.8g Fat, 182.6 Calories

Baked Calamari And Shrimp

Serves: 1
Cooking Time: 20 Minutes
Ingredients:
- 8 ounces calamari, cut in medium rings
- 7 ounces shrimp, peeled and deveined
- 1 eggs
- 3 tablespoons coconut flour
- 1 tablespoon coconut oil
- 2 tablespoons avocado, chopped
- 1 teaspoon tomato paste
- 1 tablespoon mayonnaise
- A splash of Worcestershire sauce
- 1 teaspoon lemon juice
- 2 lemon slices
- Salt and black pepper to the taste
- ½ teaspoon turmeric

Directions:
1. In a bowl, whisk egg with coconut oil.
2. Add calamari rings and shrimp and toss to coat.
3. In another bowl, mix flour with salt, pepper and turmeric and stir.
4. Dredge calamari and shrimp in this mix, place everything on a lined baking sheet, introduce in the oven at 400 °F and bake for 10 minutes.
5. Flip calamari and shrimp and bake for 10 minutes more.
6. Meanwhile, in a bowl, mix avocado with mayo and tomato paste and mash using a fork.
7. Add Worcestershire sauce, lemon juice, salt and pepper and stir well.
8. Divide baked calamari and shrimp on plates and serve with the sauce and lemon juice on the side.
9. Enjoy!

Nutrition Info:
- 10 carbs; 34 protein; 23 fat; 368 calories

Flounder With Dill And Capers

Servings: 4
Cooking Time: 15 Minutes
Ingredients:
- 4 flounder fillets
- 1 tbsp. chopped fresh dill
- 2 tbsp. capers, chopped
- 4 lemon wedges
- 6 tbsp olive oil
- Salt and pepper to taste

Directions:
1. Place a trivet in a large saucepan and pour a cup or two of water into the pan. Bring to a boil.
2. Place flounder in a heatproof dish that fits inside a saucepan. Season snapper with pepper and salt. Drizzle with olive oil on all sides. Sprinkle dill and capers on top of the filet.
3. Seal dish with foil. Place the dish on the trivet inside the saucepan. Cover and steam for 15 minutes.
4. Serve and enjoy with lemon wedges.

Nutrition Info:
- Per Servings 8.6g Carbs, 20.3g Protein, 35.9g Fat, 447 Calories

Mustard-crusted Salmon

Servings: 4
Cooking Time: 15 Minutes
Ingredients:
- 1 ¼ lb. salmon fillets, cut into 4 portions
- 2 tsp. lemon juice
- 2 tbsp. stone-ground mustard
- Lemon wedges, for garnish
- 4 tbsp olive oil
- Salt and pepper to taste

Directions:
1. Place a trivet in a large saucepan and pour a cup of water into the pan. Bring to a boil.
2. Place salmon in a heatproof dish that fits inside saucepan and drizzle with olive oil. Season the salmon fillets with salt, pepper, and lemon juice. Sprinkle with mustard on top and garnish with lemon wedges on top. Seal dish with foil.
3. Place the dish on the trivet inside the saucepan. Cover and steam for 15 minutes.
4. Serve and enjoy.

Nutrition Info:
- Per Servings 2.9g Carbs, 29g Protein, 24.8g Fat, 360 Calories

Bacon And Salmon Bites

Serves: 2
Cooking Time: 15 Minutes
Ingredients:
- 1 salmon fillets
- 4 bacon slices, halved
- 2 tbsp chopped cilantro
- Seasoning:
- ¼ tsp salt
- 1/8 tsp ground black pepper

Directions:
1. Turn on the oven, then set it to 350 °F, and let it preheat.Meanwhile, cut salmon into bite-size pieces, then wrap each piece with a half slice of bacon, secure with a toothpick and season with salt and black pepper. Take a baking sheet, place prepared salmon pieces on it and bake for 13 to 15 minutes until nicely browned and thoroughly cooked.When done, sprinkle cilantro over salmon and serve.

Nutrition Info:
- 1 g Carbs; 10 g Protein; 9 g Fats; 120 Calories

Coconut Crab Patties

Servings: 8
Cooking Time: 15 Minutes
Ingredients:
- 2 tbsp coconut oil
- 1 tbsp lemon juice
- 1 cup lump crab meat
- 2 tsp Dijon mustard
- 1 egg, beaten
- 1 ½ tbsp coconut flour

Directions:
1. In a bowl to the crabmeat add all the ingredients, except for the oil; mix well to combine. Make patties out of the mixture. Melt the coconut oil in a skillet over medium heat. Add the crab patties and cook for about 2-3 minutes per side.

Nutrition Info:
- Per Servings 3.6g Carbs, 15.3g Protein, 11.5g Fat, 215 Calories

Chili-lime Shrimps

Servings: 4
Cooking Time: 10 Minutes
Ingredients:
- 1 ½ lb. raw shrimp, peeled and deveined
- 1 tbsp. chili flakes
- 5 tbsp sweet chili sauce
- 2 tbsp. lime juice, freshly squeezed
- 1 tsp cayenne pepper
- Salt and pepper to taste
- 5 tbsp oil
- 3 tbsp water

Directions:
1. In a small bowl, whisk well chili flakes, sweet chili sauce, cayenne pepper, and water.
2. On medium-high fire, heat a nonstick saucepan for 2 minutes. Add oil to a pan and swirl to coat bottom and sides. Heat oil for a minute.
3. Stir fry shrimp, around 5 minutes. Season lightly with salt and pepper.
4. Stir in sweet chili mixture and toss well shrimp to coat.
5. Turn off fire, drizzle lime juice and toss well to coat.
6. Serve and enjoy.

Nutrition Info:
- Per Servings 1.7g Carbs, 34.9g Protein, 19.8g Fat, 306 Calories

Sauces And Dressing Recipes

Sauces And Dressing Recipes

Keto Ranch Dip

Servings: 8
Cooking Time: 10 Minutes
Ingredients:
- 1 cup egg white, beaten
- 1 lemon juice, freshly squeezed
- Salt and pepper to taste
- 1 teaspoon mustard paste
- 1 cup olive oil
- Salt and pepper to taste

Directions:
1. Add all ingredients to a pot and bring to a simmer. Stir frequently.
2. Simmer for 10 minutes.
3. Adjust seasoning to taste.

Nutrition Info:
- Per Servings 1.2g Carbs, 3.4g Protein, 27.1g Fat, 258 Calories

Ketogenic-friendly Gravy

Servings: 6
Cooking Time: 10 Minutes
Ingredients:
- 2 tablespoons butter
- 1 white onion, chopped
- ¼ cup coconut milk
- 2 cups bone broth
- 1 tablespoon balsamic vinegar
- Salt and pepper to taste

Directions:
1. Add all ingredients to a pot and bring to a simmer. Stir frequently.
2. Simmer for 10 minutes.
3. Adjust seasoning to taste.

Nutrition Info:
- Per Servings 1.1g Carbs, 0.2g Protein, 6.3g Fat, 59 Calories

Roasted Garlic Lemon Dip

Servings: 3
Cooking Time: 30 Minutes
Ingredients:
- 3 medium lemons
- 3 cloves garlic, peeled and smashed
- 5 tablespoons olive oil, divided
- 1/2 teaspoon kosher salt
- Pepper to taste
- Salt
- Pepper

Directions:
1. Arrange a rack in the middle of the oven and heat to 400°F.
2. Cut the lemons in half crosswise and remove the seeds. Place the lemons cut-side up in a small baking dish. Add the garlic and drizzle with 2 tablespoons of the oil.
3. Roast until the lemons are tender and lightly browned, about 30 minutes. Remove the baking dish to a wire rack.
4. When the lemons are cool enough to handle, squeeze the juice into the baking dish. Discard the lemon pieces and any remaining seeds. Pour the contents of the baking dish, including the garlic, into a blender or mini food processor. Add the remaining 3 tablespoons oil and salt. Process until the garlic is completely puréed, and the sauce is emulsified and slightly thickened. Serve warm or at room temperature.

Nutrition Info:
- Per Servings 4.8g Carbs, 0.6g Protein, 17g Fat, 165 Calories

Dijon Vinaigrette

Servings: 4
Cooking Time: 5 Minutes
Ingredients:
- 2 tablespoons Dijon mustard
- Juice of ½ lemon
- 1 garlic clove, finely minced
- 1½ tablespoons red wine vinegar
- Pink Himalayan salt
- Freshly ground black pepper
- 3 tablespoons olive oil

Directions:
1. In a small bowl, whisk the mustard, lemon juice, garlic, and red wine vinegar until well combined. Season with pink Himalayan salt and pepper, and whisk

again.

2. Slowly add the olive oil, a little bit at a time, whisking constantly.

3. Keep in a sealed glass container in the refrigerator for up to 1 week.

Nutrition Info:

- Per Servings 1g Carbs, 1g Protein, 11g Fat, 99 Calories

Caesar Dressing

Servings: 4
Cooking Time: 5 Minutes

Ingredients:

- ½ cup mayonnaise
- 1 tablespoon Dijon mustard
- Juice of ½ lemon
- ½ teaspoon Worcestershire sauce
- Pinch pink Himalayan salt
- Pinch freshly ground black pepper
- ¼ cup grated Parmesan cheese

Directions:

1. In a medium bowl, whisk together the mayonnaise, mustard, lemon juice, Worcestershire sauce, pink Himalayan salt, and pepper until fully combined.

2. Add the Parmesan cheese, and whisk until creamy and well blended.

3. Keep in a sealed glass container in the refrigerator for up to 1 week.

Nutrition Info:

- Per Servings Calories: 2g Carbs, 2g Protein, 23g Fat, 222 Calories

Keto Thousand Island Dressing

Servings: 10
Cooking Time: 10 Minutes

Ingredients:

- 1 cup mayonnaise
- 1 tablespoon lemon juice, freshly squeezed
- 4 tablespoons dill pickles, chopped
- 1 teaspoon Tabasco
- 1 shallot chopped finely
- Salt and pepper to taste

Directions:

1. Add all ingredients to a pot and bring to a simmer. Stir frequently.

2. Simmer for 10 minutes.

3. Adjust seasoning to taste.

Nutrition Info:

- Per Servings 2.3g Carbs, 1.7g Protein, 7.8g Fat, 85 Calories

Avocado-lime Crema

Servings: 4
Cooking Time: 5 Minutes

Ingredients:

- ½ cup sour cream
- ½ avocado
- 1 garlic clove, finely minced
- ¼ cup fresh cilantro leaves
- Juice of ½ lime
- Pinch pink Himalayan salt
- Pinch freshly ground black pepper

Directions:

1. In a food processor (or blender), mix the sour cream, avocado, garlic, cilantro, lime juice, pink Himalayan salt, and pepper until smooth and fully combined.

2. Spoon the sauce into an airtight glass jar and keep in the refrigerator for up to 3 days.

Nutrition Info:

- Per Servings Calories: 2g Carbs, 1g Protein, 8g Fat, 87 Calories

Cheesy Avocado Dip

Servings:
Cooking Time: 20 Minutes

Ingredients:

- 1/2 medium ripe avocado, peeled and pitted
- 2 crumbled blue cheese
- 1 freshly squeezed lemon juice
- 1/2 kosher salt
- 1/2 cup water

Directions:

1. Scoop the flesh of the avocado into the bowl of a food processor fitted with the blade attachment or blender.

2. Add the blue cheese, lemon juice, and salt. Blend until smooth and creamy, 30 to 40 seconds.

3. With the motor running, add the water and blend until the sauce is thinned and well-combined.

Nutrition Info:

- Per Servings 2.9g Carbs, 3.5g Protein, 7.2g Fat, 86 Calories

Caesar Salad Dressing

Servings: 6
Cooking Time: 10 Minutes

Ingredients:
- ½ cup olive oil
- 1 tablespoon Dijon mustard
- ½ cup parmesan cheese, grated
- 2/3-ounce anchovies, chopped
- ½ lemon juice, freshly squeezed
- Salt and pepper to taste

Directions:
1. Add all ingredients to a pot and bring to a simmer. Stir frequently.
2. Simmer for 10 minutes.
3. Adjust seasoning to taste.

Nutrition Info:
- Per Servings 1.5g Carbs, 3.4g Protein, 20.7g Fat, 203 Calories

Green Jalapeno Sauce

Servings: 1
Cooking Time: 0 Minutes

Ingredients:
- ½ avocado
- 1 large jalapeno
- 1 cup fresh cilantro
- 2 tablespoons extra virgin olive oil
- 3 tablespoons water
- Water
- ½ teaspoon salt

Directions:
1. Add all ingredients in a blender.
2. Blend until smooth and creamy.
3. Serve and enjoy.

Nutrition Info:
- Per Servings 10g Carbs, 2.4g Protein, 42g Fat, 407 Calories

Tzatziki

Servings: 4
Cooking Time: 10 Minutes, Plus At Least 30 Minutes To Chill

Ingredients:
- ½ large English cucumber, unpeeled
- 1½ cups Greek yogurt (I use Fage)
- 2 tablespoons olive oil
- Large pinch pink Himalayan salt
- Large pinch freshly ground black pepper
- Juice of ½ lemon
- 2 garlic cloves, finely minced
- 1 tablespoon fresh dill

Directions:
1. Halve the cucumber lengthwise, and use a spoon to scoop out and discard the seeds.
2. Grate the cucumber with a zester or grater onto a large plate lined with a few layers of paper towels. Close the paper towels around the grated cucumber, and squeeze as much water out of it as you can. (This can take a while and can require multiple paper towels. You can also allow it to drain overnight in a strainer or wrapped in a few layers of cheesecloth in the fridge if you have the time.)
3. In a food processor (or blender), blend the yogurt, olive oil, pink Himalayan salt, pepper, lemon juice, and garlic until fully combined.
4. Transfer the mixture to a medium bowl, and mix in the fresh dill and grated cucumber.
5. I like to chill this sauce for at least 30 minutes before serving. Keep in a sealed glass container in the refrigerator for up to 1 week.

Nutrition Info:
- Per Servings 5g Carbs, 8g Protein, 11g Fat, 149 Calories

Celery-onion Vinaigrette

Servings: 4
Cooking Time: 0 Minutes

Ingredients:
- 1 tbsp finely chopped celery
- 1 tbsp finely chopped red onion
- 4 garlic cloves, minced
- ½ cup red wine vinegar
- 1 tbsp extra virgin olive oil

Directions:
1. Prepare the dressing by mixing pepper, celery, onion, olive oil, garlic, and vinegar in a small bowl. Whisk well to combine.
2. Let it sit for at least 30 minutes to let flavors blend.
3. Serve and enjoy with your favorite salad greens.

Nutrition Info:
- Per Servings 1.4g Carbs, 0.2g Protein, 3.4g Fat, 41 Calories

Feta Avocado Dip

Servings: 4

Cooking Time: 0 Minutes

Ingredients:
- 2 avocadoes (mashed)
- ½ cup feta cheese (crumbled)
- 1 plum tomatoes (diced)
- 1 teaspoon garlic (minced)
- ½ lemon (juiced)
- Salt
- Pepper
- 4 tablespoons olive oil

Directions:

1. Fold ingredients together. Do not stir too much to leave chunks of feta and avocado.

2. Serve and enjoy.

Nutrition Info:
- Per Servings 8.1g Carbs, 5g Protein, 19g Fat, 220 Calories

Vegetarian Fish Sauce

Servings: 16

Cooking Time: 20 Minutes

Ingredients:
- 1/4 cup dried shiitake mushrooms
- 1-2 tbsp tamari (for a depth of flavor)
- 3 tbsp coconut aminos
- 1 ¼ cup water
- 2 tsp sea salt

Directions:

1. To a small saucepan, add water, coconut aminos, dried shiitake mushrooms, and sea salt. Bring to a boil, then cover, reduce heat, and simmer for 15-20 minutes.

2. Remove from heat and let cool slightly. Pour liquid through a fine-mesh strainer into a bowl, pressing on the mushroom mixture with a spoon to squeeze out any remaining liquid.

3. To the bowl, add tamari. Taste and adjust as needed, adding more sea salt for saltiness.

4. Store in a sealed container in the refrigerator for up to 1 month and shake well before use. Or pour into an ice cube tray, freeze, and store in a freezer-safe container for up to 2 months.

Nutrition Info:
- Per Servings 5g Carbs, 0.3g Protein, 2g Fat, 39.1 Calories

Cowboy Sauce

Servings: 6

Cooking Time: 10 Minutes

Ingredients:
- 1 stick butter
- 2 cloves of garlic, minced
- 1 tablespoon fresh horseradish, grated
- 1 teaspoon dried thyme
- 1 teaspoon paprika powder
- Salt and pepper to taste
- ¼ cup water

Directions:

1. Add all ingredients to a pot and bring to a simmer.

2. Simmer for 10 minutes.

3. Adjust seasoning to taste.

Nutrition Info:
- Per Servings 0.9g Carbs, 1.3g Protein, 20.6g Fat, 194 Calories

Peanut Sauce

Servings: 4

Cooking Time: 5 Minutes

Ingredients:
- ½ cup creamy peanut butter (I use Justin's)
- 2 tablespoons soy sauce (or coconut aminos)
- 1 teaspoon Sriracha sauce
- 1 teaspoon toasted sesame oil
- 1 teaspoon garlic powder

Directions:

1. In a food processor (or blender), blend the peanut butter, soy sauce, Sriracha sauce, sesame oil, and garlic powder until thoroughly mixed.

2. Pour into an airtight glass container and keep in the refrigerator for up to 1 week.

Nutrition Info:
- Per Servings Calories: 185; Total Fat: 15g; Carbs: 8g; Net Carbs: 6g; Fiber: 2g; Protein: 7g

Simple Tomato Sauce

Servings: 4

Cooking Time: 20 Minutes

Ingredients:
- 1 can whole peeled tomatoes
- 3 garlic cloves, smashed
- 5 tablespoons olive oil
- Kosher salt
- 2 tablespoons unsalted butter
- Salt

Directions:

1. Purée tomatoes in a food processor until they're as smooth or chunky as you like.
2. Transfer tomatoes to a large Dutch oven or other heavy pot. (Or, use an immersion blender and blend directly in the pot.)
3. Add garlic, oil, and a 5-finger pinch of salt.
4. Bring to a boil and cook, occasionally stirring, until sauce is reduced by about one-third, about 20 minutes. Stir in butter.

Nutrition Info:

• Per Servings 7.6g Carbs, 1.9g Protein, 21.3g Fat, 219 Calories

Alfredo Sauce

Servings: 2
Cooking Time: 10 Minutes

Ingredients:

• 4 tablespoons butter
• 2 ounces cream cheese
• 1 cup heavy (whipping) cream
• ½ cup grated Parmesan cheese
• 1 garlic clove, finely minced
• 1 teaspoon dried Italian seasoning
• Pink Himalayan salt
• Freshly ground black pepper

Directions:

1. In a heavy medium saucepan over medium heat, combine the butter, cream cheese, and heavy cream. Whisk slowly and constantly until the butter and cream cheese melt.
2. Add the Parmesan, garlic, and Italian seasoning. Continue to whisk until everything is well blended. Turn the heat to medium-low and simmer, stirring occasionally, for 5 to 8 minutes to allow the sauce to blend and thicken.
3. Season with pink Himalayan salt and pepper, and stir to combine.
4. Toss with your favorite hot, precooked, keto-friendly noodles and serve.
5. Keep this sauce in a sealed glass container in the refrigerator for up to 4 days.

Nutrition Info:

• Per Servings 2g Carbs, 5g Protein, 30g Fat, 294 Calories

Artichoke Pesto Dip

Servings: 1
Cooking Time: 20 Minutes

Ingredients:

• 1 jar marinated artichoke hearts
• 8 ounces cream cheese (at room temperature)
• 4 ounces parmesan cheese (grated)
• 2 tablespoons basil pesto
• ¼ cup shelled pistachio (chopped, optional)

Directions:

1. Preheat oven to 375oF.
2. Drain and chop artichoke hearts.
3. Mix artichokes, cream cheese, parmesan, and pesto.
4. Pour into 4 ramekins evenly.
5. Bake for 15-20 minutes.

Nutrition Info:

• Per Servings 5g Carbs, 8g Protein, 19g Fat, 214 Calories

Fat-burning Dressing

Servings: 6
Cooking Time: 3 Minutes

Ingredients:

• 2 tablespoons coconut oil
• ¼ cup olive oil
• 2 cloves of garlic, minced
• 2 tablespoons freshly chopped herbs of your choice
• ¼ cup mayonnaise
• Salt and pepper to taste

Directions:

1. Heat the coconut oil and olive oil and sauté the garlic until fragrant in a saucepan.
2. Allow cooling slightly before adding the mayonnaise.
3. Season with salt and pepper to taste.

Nutrition Info:

• Per Servings 0.6g Carbs, 14.1g Protein, 22.5g Fat, 262 Calories

Green Goddess Dressing

Servings: 4
Cooking Time: 5 Minutes

Ingredients:

• 2 tablespoon buttermilk
• ¼ cup Greek yogurt
• 1 teaspoon apple cider vinegar
• 1 garlic clove, minced
• 1 tablespoon olive oil

- 1 tablespoon fresh parsley leaves

Directions:

1. In a food processor (or blender), combine the buttermilk, yogurt, apple cider vinegar, garlic, olive oil, and parsley. Blend until fully combined.

2. Pour into a sealed glass container and chill in the refrigerator for at least 30 minutes before serving. This dressing will keep in the fridge for up to 1 week.

Nutrition Info:

- Per Servings 1g Carbs, 1g Protein, 6g Fat, 62 Calories

Garlic Aioli

Servings: 4

Cooking Time: 5 Minutes, Plus 30 Minutes To Chill

Ingredients:

- ½ cup mayonnaise
- 2 garlic cloves, minced
- Juice of 1 lemon
- 1 tablespoon chopped fresh flat-leaf Italian parsley
- 1 teaspoon chopped chives
- Pink Himalayan salt
- Freshly ground black pepper

Directions:

1. In a food processor (or blender), combine the mayonnaise, garlic, lemon juice, parsley, and chives, and season with pink Himalayan salt and pepper. Blend until fully combined.

2. Pour into a sealed glass container and chill in the refrigerator for at least 30 minutes before serving. (This sauce will keep in the fridge for up to 1 week.)

Nutrition Info:

- Per Servings Calories: 3g Carbs, 1g Protein, 22g Fat, 204 Calories

Sriracha Mayo

Servings: 4

Cooking Time: 5 Minutes

Ingredients:

- ½ cup mayonnaise
- 2 tablespoons Sriracha sauce
- ½ teaspoon garlic powder
- ½ teaspoon onion powder
- ¼ teaspoon paprika

Directions:

1. In a small bowl, whisk together the mayonnaise, Sriracha, garlic powder, onion powder, and paprika until well mixed.

2. Pour into an airtight glass container, and keep in the refrigerator for up to 1 week.

Nutrition Info:

- Per Servings Calories: 2g Carbs, 1g Protein, 22g Fat, 201 Calories

Lemon Tahini Sauce

Servings: 2

Cooking Time: 5 Minutes

Ingredients:

- 1/2 cup packed fresh herbs, such as parsley, basil, mint, cilantro, dill, or chives
- 1/4 cup tahini
- Juice of 1 lemon
- 1/2 teaspoon kosher salt
- 1 tablespoon water

Directions:

1. Place all the ingredients in the bowl of a food processor fitted with the blade attachment or a blender. Process continuously until the herbs are finely minced, and the sauce is well-blended, 3 to 4 minutes.

2. Serve immediately or store in a covered container in the refrigerator until ready to serve.

Nutrition Info:

- Per Servings 4.3g Carbs, 2.8g Protein, 8.1g Fat, 94 Calories

Chunky Blue Cheese Dressing

Servings: 4

Cooking Time: 5 Minutes

Ingredients:

- ½ cup sour cream
- ½ cup mayonnaise
- Juice of ½ lemon
- ½ teaspoon Worcestershire sauce
- Pink Himalayan salt
- Freshly ground black pepper
- 2 ounces crumbled blue cheese

Directions:

1. In a medium bowl, whisk the sour cream, mayonnaise, lemon juice, and Worcestershire sauce. Season with pink Himalayan salt and pepper, and whisk again until fully combined.

2. Fold in the crumbled blue cheese until well combined.

3. Keep in a sealed glass container in the refrigerator for up to 1 week.

Nutrition Info:

- Per Servings 3g Carbs, 7g Protein, 32g Fat, 306 Calories

Buttery Dijon Sauce

Servings: 2
Cooking Time: 0 Minutes

Ingredients:
- 3 parts brown butter
- 1-part vinegar or citrus juice or a combo
- 1-part strong Dijon mustard
- A small handful of flat-leaf parsley (optional)
- 3/4 teaspoon freshly ground pepper
- 1 teaspoon salt

Directions:
1. Add everything to a food processor and blitz until just smooth.
2. You can also mix this up with an immersion blender. Use immediately or store in the refrigerator for up to one day. Blend again before use.

Nutrition Info:
- Per Servings 0.7g Carbs, 0.4g Protein, 34.4g Fat, 306 Calories

Buffalo Sauce

Servings: 8
Cooking Time: 30 Minutes

Ingredients:
- 8 ounces Cream Cheese (softened)
- ½ cup Buffalo Wing Sauce
- ½ cup Blue Cheese Dressing
- 1 ½ cups Cheddar Cheese (Shredded)
- 1 ¼ cups Chicken Breast (Cooked)

Directions:
1. Preheat oven to 350oF.
2. Blend together buffalo sauce, white salad dressing, cream cheese, chicken, and shredded cheese.
3. Top with any other optional ingredients like blue cheese chunks.
4. Bake for 25-30 minutes

Nutrition Info:
- Per Servings 2.2g Carbs, 16g Protein, 28g Fat, 325 Calories

Avocado Mayo

Servings: 4
Cooking Time: 5 Minutes

Ingredients:
- 1 medium avocado, cut into chunks
- ½ teaspoon ground cayenne pepper
- Juice of ½ lime
- 2 tablespoons fresh cilantro leaves (optional)
- Pinch pink Himalayan salt
- ¼ cup olive oil

Directions:
1. In a food processor (or blender), blend the avocado, cayenne pepper, lime juice, cilantro, and pink Himalayan salt until all the ingredients are well combined and smooth.
2. Slowly incorporate the olive oil, adding 1 tablespoon at a time, pulsing the food processor in between.
3. Keep in a sealed glass container in the refrigerator for up to 1 week.

Nutrition Info:
- Per Servings 1g Carbs, 1g Protein, 5g Fat, 58 Calories

Greek Yogurt Dressing

Servings: 2
Cooking Time: 0 Minutes

Ingredients:
- ¼ tsp ground ginger
- ½ tsp prepared mustard
- 2 tbsp low-fat mayonnaise
- ½ cup plain Greek yogurt
- Salt and pepper to taste

Directions:
1. In a bowl, whisk well all ingredients.
2. Adjust seasoning to taste.
3. Serve and enjoy with your favorite salad greens.

Nutrition Info:
- Per Servings 3.5g Carbs, 3.0g Protein, 2.8g Fat, 51 Calories

Desserts And Drinks Recipes

Desserts And Drinks Recipes

Brownie Mug Cake

Servings: 1
Cooking Time: 5 Minutes

Ingredients:
- 1 egg, beaten
- ¼ cup almond flour
- ¼ teaspoon baking powder
- 1 ½ tablespoons cacao powder
- 2 tablespoons stevia powder
- A pinch of salt
- 1 teaspoon cinnamon powder
- ¼ teaspoon vanilla extract (optional)

Directions:
1. Combine all ingredients in a bowl until well-combined.
2. Transfer in a heat-proof mug.
3. Place the mug in a microwave.
4. Cook for 2 minutes. Let it sit for another 2 minutes to continue cooking.
5. Serve and enjoy.

Nutrition Info:
- Per Servings 4.1g Carbs, 9.1g Protein, 11.8g Fat, 159 Calories

Chocolate Bark With Almonds

Servings: 12
Cooking Time: 1 Hour 15 Minutes

Ingredients:
- ½ cup toasted almonds, chopped
- ½ cup butter
- 10 drops stevia
- ¼ tsp salt
- ½ cup unsweetened coconut flakes
- 4 ounces dark chocolate

Directions:
1. Melt together the butter and chocolate, in the microwave, for 90 seconds. Remove and stir in stevia.
2. Line a cookie sheet with waxed paper and spread the chocolate evenly. Scatter the almonds on top, coconut flakes, and sprinkle with salt. Refrigerate for one hour.

Nutrition Info:
- Per Servings 1.9g Carbs, 1.9g Protein, 15.3g Fat, 161 Calories

Brownies With Coco Milk

Servings: 10
Cooking Time: 6 Hours

Ingredients:
- ¾ cup coconut milk
- 1 teaspoon erythritol
- 2 tablespoons butter, melted
- 4 egg yolks, beaten
- 5 tablespoons cacao powder

Directions:
1. In a bowl, mix well all ingredients.
2. Lightly grease your slow cooker with cooking spray and pour in batter.
3. Cover and cook on low for six hours.
4. Serve and enjoy.

Nutrition Info:
- Per Servings 1.2g Carbs, 1.5g Protein, 8.4g Fat, 86 Calories

Coconut Fat Bombs

Servings: 4
Cooking Time: 22 Minutes +cooling Time

Ingredients:
- 2/3 cup coconut oil, melted
- 1 can coconut milk
- 18 drops stevia liquid
- 1 cup unsweetened coconut flakes

Directions:
1. Mix the coconut oil with the milk and stevia to combine. Stir in the coconut flakes until well distributed. Pour into silicone muffin molds and freeze for 1 hour to harden.

Nutrition Info:
- Per Servings 2g Carbs, 4g Protein, 19g Fat, 214 Calories

No Nuts Fudge

Servings: 15
Cooking Time: 4 Hours
Ingredients:
- ¼ cup cocoa powder
- ½ teaspoon baking powder
- 1 stick of butter, melted
- 4 tablespoons erythritol
- 6 eggs, beaten
- Salt to taste.

Directions:
1. Mix all ingredients in a slow cooker.
2. Add a pinch of salt.
3. Mix until well combined.
4. Cover pot.
5. Press the low settings and adjust the time to 4 hours.

Nutrition Info:
- Per Servings 1.3g Carbs, 4.3g Protein, 12.2g Fat, 132 Calories

Smarties Cookies

Servings: 8
Cooking Time: 10 Mins
Ingredients:
- 1/4 cup. butter
- 1/2 cup. almond flour
- 1 tsp. vanilla essence
- 12 oz. bag of smarties
- 1 cup. stevia
- 1/4 tsp. baking powder

Directions:
1. Sift in flour and baking powder in a bowl, then stir through butter and mix until well combined.
2. Whisk in stevia and vanilla essence , stir until thick.
3. Then add the smarties and use your hand to mix and divide into small balls.
4. Bake until completely cooked, about 10 minutes. Let it cool and serve.

Nutrition Info:
- Per Servings 20.77g Carbs, 3.7g Protein, 11.89g Fat, 239 Calories

Vanilla Bean Frappuccino

Servings: 4
Cooking Time: 6 Minutes
Ingredients:
- 3 cups unsweetened vanilla almond milk, chilled
- 2 tsp swerve
- 1 ½ cups heavy cream, cold
- 1 vanilla bean
- ¼ tsp xanthan gum
- Unsweetened chocolate shavings to garnish

Directions:
1. Combine the almond milk, swerve, heavy cream, vanilla bean, and xanthan gum in the blender, and process on high speed for 1 minute until smooth. Pour into tall shake glasses, sprinkle with chocolate shavings, and serve immediately.

Nutrition Info:
- Per Servings 6g Carbs, 15g Protein, 14g Fat, 193 Calories

White Choco Fatty Fudge

Servings: 6
Cooking Time: 10 Minutes
Ingredients:
- 1/4 cup coconut butter
- 1/4 cup cashew butter
- 2 tbsp cacao butter
- 1/4 teaspoon vanilla powder
- 10–12 drops liquid stevia, or to taste
- 2 tbsp coconut oil

Directions:
1. Over low heat, place a small saucepan and melt coconut oil, cacao butter, cashew butter, and coconut butter.
2. Remove from the heat and stir in the vanilla and stevia.
3. Pour into a silicone mold and place it in the freezer for 30 minutes.
4. Store in the fridge for a softer consistency.

Nutrition Info:
- Per Servings 1.7g Carbs, 0.2g Protein, 23.7g Fat, 221 Calories

Cinnamon Cookies

Servings: 4
Cooking Time: 25 Minutes

Ingredients:
- 2 cups almond flour
- ½ tsp baking soda
- ¾ cup sweetener
- ½ cup butter, softened
- A pinch of salt
- Coating:
- 2 tbsp erythritol sweetener
- 1 tsp cinnamon

Directions:
1. Preheat your oven to 350ºF. Combine all cookie ingredients in a bowl. Make 16 balls out of the mixture and flatten them with hands. Combine the cinnamon and erythritol. Dip the cookies in the cinnamon mixture and arrange them on a lined cookie sheet. Cook for 15 minutes, until crispy.

Nutrition Info:
- Per Servings 1.5g Carbs, 3g Protein, 13g Fat, 131 Calories

Coconut Raspberry Bars

Servings: 12
Cooking Time: 20 Minutes

Ingredients:
- 1 cup coconut milk
- 3 cups desiccated coconut
- 1/3 cup erythritol powder
- 1 cup raspberries, pulsed
- ½ cup coconut oil or other oils

Directions:
1. Preheat oven to 380oF.
2. Combine all ingredients in a mixing bowl.
3. Pour into a greased baking dish.
4. Bake in the oven for 20 minutes.
5. Let it rest for 10 minutes.
6. Serve and enjoy.

Nutrition Info:
- Per Servings 8.2g Carbs, 1.5g Protein, 14.7g Fat, 170 Calories

Green And Fruity Smoothie

Servings: 2
Cooking Time: 0 Minutes

Ingredients:
- 1 cup spinach, packed
- ½ cup strawberries, chopped
- ½ avocado, peeled, pitted, and frozen
- 1 tbsp almond butter
- ¼ cup packed kale, stem discarded, and leaves chopped
- 1 cup ice-cold water
- 5 tablespoons MCT oil or coconut oil

Directions:
1. Blend all ingredients in a blender until smooth and creamy.
2. Serve and enjoy.

Nutrition Info:
- Per Servings 10g Carbs, 1.6g Protein, 47.3g Fat, 459 Calories

Coconut-melon Yogurt Shake

Servings: 1
Cooking Time: 0 Minutes

Ingredients:
- ¼ cup half and half
- 3 tbsp coconut oil
- ½ cup melon, slices
- 1 tbsp coconut flakes, unsweetened
- 1 tbsp chia seeds
- 1 ½ cups water
- 1 packet Stevia, or more to taste

Directions:
1. Add all ingredients in a blender.
2. Blend until smooth and creamy.
3. Serve and enjoy.

Nutrition Info:
- Per Servings 8g Carbs, 2.4g Protein, 43g Fat, 440 Calories

Baby Kale And Yogurt Smoothie

Servings: 1

Cooking Time: 0 Minutes

Ingredients:

- ½ cup whole milk yogurt
- ½ cup baby kale greens
- 1 packet Stevia, or more to taste
- 3 tbsps MCT oil
- ½ tbsp sunflower seeds
- 1 cup water

Directions:

1. Add all ingredients in a blender.
2. Blend until smooth and creamy.
3. Serve and enjoy.

Nutrition Info:

- Per Servings 2.6g Carbs, 11.0g Protein, 26.2g Fat, 329 Calories

Choco Coffee Milk Shake

Servings: 1

Cooking Time: 0 Minutes

Ingredients:

- ½ cup coconut milk
- 1 tbsp cocoa powder
- 1 cup brewed coffee, chilled
- 1 packet Stevia, or more to taste
- ½ tsp cinnamon
- 5 tbsps coconut oil

Directions:

1. Add all ingredients in a blender.
2. Blend until smooth and creamy.
3. Serve and enjoy.

Nutrition Info:

- Per Servings 10g Carbs, 4.1g Protein, 97.4g Fat, 880 Calories

White Chocolate Cheesecake Bites

Servings: 12

Cooking Time: 4 Minutes + Cooling Time

Ingredients:

- 10 oz unsweetened white chocolate chips
- ½ half and half
- 20 oz cream cheese, softened
- ½ cup swerve
- 1 tsp vanilla extract

Directions:

1. In a saucepan, melt the chocolate with half and a half on low heat for 1 minute. Turn the heat off.

2. In a bowl, whisk the cream cheese, swerve, and vanilla extract with a hand mixer until smooth. Stir into the chocolate mixture. Spoon into silicone muffin tins and freeze for 4 hours until firm.

Nutrition Info:

- Per Servings 3.1g Carbs, 5g Protein, 22g Fat, 241 Calories

Crispy Zucchini Chips

Servings: 5

Cooking Time: 20 Mins

Ingredients:

- 1 large egg, beaten
- 1 cup. almond flour
- 1 medium zucchini, thinly sliced
- 3/4 cup Parmesan cheese, grated
- Cooking spray

Directions:

1. Preheat oven to 400 degrees F. Line a baking pan with parchment paper.
2. In a bowl, mix together Parmesan cheese and almond flour.
3. In another bowl whisk the egg. Dip each zucchini slice in the egg, then the cheese mixture until finely coated.
4. Spray zucchini slices with cooking spray and place in the prepared oven.
5. Bake for 20 minutes until crispy. Serve.

Nutrition Info:

- Per Servings 16.8g Carbs, 10.8g Protein, 6g Fat, 215.2 Calories

Blackberry Cheese Vanilla Blocks

Servings: 5

Cooking Time: 20mins

Ingredients:

- ½ cup blackberries
- 6 eggs
- 4 oz mascarpone cheese
- 1 tsp vanilla extract
- 4 tbsp stevia
- 8 oz melted coconut oil
- ½ tsp baking powder

Directions:

1. Except for blackberries, blend all ingredients in a blender until smooth.
2. Combine blackberries with blended mixture and transfer to a baking dish.

3. Bake blackberries mixture in the oven at 320°F for 20 minutes. Serve.

Nutrition Info:
- Per Servings 15g Carbs, 13g Protein, 4g Fat, 199 Calories

Berry Tart

Servings: 4
Cooking Time: 45 Minutes

Ingredients:
- 4 eggs
- 2 tsp coconut oil
- 2 cups berries
- 1 cup coconut milk
- 1 cup almond flour
- ¼ cup sweetener
- ½ tsp vanilla powder
- 1 tbsp powdered sweetener
- A pinch of salt

Directions:
1. Preheat the oven to 350ºF. Place all ingredients except coconut oil, berries, and powdered sweetener, in a blender; blend until smooth. Gently fold in the berries. Grease a baking dish with the oil. Pour the mixture into the prepared pan and bake for 35 minutes. Sprinkle with powdered sugar to serve.

Nutrition Info:
- Per Servings 4.9g Carbs, 15g Protein, 26.5g Fat, 305 Calories

Creamy Coconut Kiwi Drink

Servings: 4
Cooking Time: 3 Minutes

Ingredients:
- 6 kiwis, pulp scooped
- 3 tbsp erythritol or to taste
- 3 cups unsweetened coconut milk
- 2 cups coconut cream
- 7 ice cubes
- Mint leaves to garnish

Directions:
1. In a blender, process the kiwis, erythritol, milk, cream, and ice cubes until smooth, about 3 minutes. Pour into four serving glasses, garnish with mint leaves, and serve.

Nutrition Info:
- Per Servings 1g Carbs, 16g Protein, 38g Fat, 425 Calories

Almond Choco Shake

Servings: 1
Cooking Time: 0 Minutes

Ingredients:
- ½ cup heavy cream, liquid
- 1 tbsp cocoa powder
- 1 packet Stevia, or more to taste
- 5 almonds, chopped
- 1 ½ cups water
- 3 tbsp coconut oil

Directions:
1. Add all ingredients in a blender.
2. Blend until smooth and creamy.
3. Serve and enjoy.

Nutrition Info:
- Per Servings 9.7g Carbs, 11.9g Protein, 45.9g Fat, 485 Calories

Dark Chocolate Mousse With Stewed Plums

Servings: 6
Cooking Time: 45 Minutes

Ingredients:
- 12 oz unsweetened chocolate
- 8 eggs, separated into yolks and whites
- 2 tbsp salt
- ¾ cup swerve sugar
- ½ cup olive oil
- 3 tbsp brewed coffee
- Stewed Plums
- 4 plums, pitted and halved
- ½ stick cinnamon
- ½ cup swerve
- ½ cup water
- ½ lemon, juiced

Directions:
1. Put the chocolate in a bowl and melt in the microwave for 1 ½ minutes. In a separate bowl, whisk the yolks with half of the swerve until a pale yellow has formed, then, beat in the salt, olive oil, and coffee. Mix in the melted chocolate until smooth.
2. In a third bowl, whisk the whites with the hand mixer until a soft peak has formed. Sprinkle the remaining swerve sugar over and gently fold in with a spatula. Fetch a tablespoon full of the chocolate mixture and fold in to combine. Pour in the remaining chocolate mixture and whisk to mix.
3. Pour the mousse into 6 ramekins, cover with plas-

tic wrap, and refrigerate overnight. The next morning, pour water, swerve, cinnamon, and lemon juice in a saucepan and bring to a simmer for 3 minutes, occasionally stirring to ensure the swerve has dissolved and a syrup has formed.

4. Add the plums and poach in the sweetened water for 18 minutes until soft. Turn the heat off and discard the cinnamon stick. Spoon a plum each with syrup on the chocolate mousse and serve.

Nutrition Info:

• Per Servings 6.9g Carbs, 9.5g Protein, 23g Fat, 288 Calories

Cardamom-cinnamon Spiced Coco-latte

Servings: 1
Cooking Time: 0 Minutes

Ingredients:

• ½ cup coconut milk
• ¼ tsp cardamom powder
• 1 tbsp chocolate powder
• 1 ½ cups brewed coffee, chilled
• 1 tbsp coconut oil
• ¼ tsp cinnamon
• ¼ tsp nutmeg

Directions:

1. Add all ingredients in a blender.
2. Blend until smooth and creamy.
3. Serve and enjoy.

Nutrition Info:

• Per Servings 7.5g Carbs, 3.8g Protein, 38.7g Fat, 362 Calories

Lychee And Coconut Lassi

Servings: 4
Cooking Time: 2 Hours 28 Minutes

Ingredients:

• 2 cups lychee pulp, seeded
• 2 ½ cups coconut milk
• 4 tsp swerve
• 2 limes, zested and juiced
• 1 ½ cups plain yogurt
• 1 lemongrass, white part only, crushed
• Toasted coconut shavings for garnish

Directions:

1. In a saucepan, add the lychee pulp, coconut milk, swerve, lemongrass, and lime zest. Stir and bring to boil on medium heat for 2 minutes, = stirring continually. Then reduce the heat, and simmer for 1 minute.

Turn the heat off and let the mixture sit for 15 minutes.

2. Remove the lemongrass and pour the mixture into a smoothie maker or a blender, add the yogurt and lime juice, and process the ingredients until smooth, for about 60 seconds.

3. Pour into a jug and refrigerate for 2 hours until cold; stir. Serve garnished with coconut shavings.

Nutrition Info:

• Per Servings 1.5g Carbs, 5.3g Protein, 26.1g Fat, 285 Calories

Strawberry Yogurt Shake

Servings: 1
Cooking Time: 0 Minutes

Ingredients:

• ½ cup whole milk yogurt
• 4 strawberries, chopped
• 1 tbsp cocoa powder
• 3 tbsp coconut oil
• 1 tbsp pepitas
• 1 ½ cups water
• 1 packet Stevia, or more to taste

Directions:

1. Add all ingredients in a blender.
2. Blend until smooth and creamy.
3. Serve and enjoy.

Nutrition Info:

• Per Servings 10.5g Carbs, 7.7g Protein, 49.3g Fat, 496 Calories

Chocolate Cakes

Servings: 6
Cooking Time: 25 Minutes

Ingredients:

• ½ cup almond flour
• ¼ cup xylitol
• 1 tsp baking powder
• ½ tsp baking soda
• 1 tsp cinnamon, ground
• A pinch of salt
• A pinch of ground cloves
• ½ cup butter, melted
• ½ cup buttermilk
• 1 egg
• 1 tsp pure almond extract
• For the Frosting:
• 1 cup double cream
• 1 cup dark chocolate, flaked

Directions:

1. Preheat the oven to 360ºF. Use a cooking spray to grease a donut pan.

2. In a bowl, mix the cloves, almond flour, baking powder, salt, baking soda, xylitol, and cinnamon. In a separate bowl, combine the almond extract, butter, egg, buttermilk, and cream. Mix the wet mixture into the dry mixture. Evenly ladle the batter into the donut pan. Bake for 17 minutes.

3. Set a pan over medium heat and warm double cream; simmer for 2 minutes. Fold in the chocolate flakes; combine until all the chocolate melts; let cool. Spread the top of the cakes with the frosting.

Nutrition Info:

• Per Servings 10g Carbs, 4.8g Protein, 20g Fat, 218 Calories

Chia And Blackberry Pudding

Servings: 2
Cooking Time: 10 Minutes

Ingredients:

• 1 cup full-fat natural yogurt
• 2 tsp swerve
• 2 tbsp chia seeds
• 1 cup fresh blackberries
• 1 tbsp lemon zest
• Mint leaves, to serve

Directions:

1. Mix together the yogurt and the swerve. Stir in the chia seeds. Reserve 4 blackberries for garnish and mash the remaining ones with a fork until pureed. Stir in the yogurt mixture

2. Chill in the fridge for 30 minutes. When cooled, divide the mixture between 2 glasses. Top each with a couple of raspberries, mint leaves, lemon zest and serve.

Nutrition Info:

• Per Servings 4.7g Carbs, 7.5g Protein, 10g Fat, 169 Calories

Choco-coco Bars

Servings: 12
Cooking Time: 10 Minutes

Ingredients:

• 1/3 cup Virgin Coconut Oil, melted
• 2 cups shredded unsweetened coconut
• 2 droppers Liquid Stevia
• 2 droppers of Liquid Stevia
• 3 squares Baker's Unsweetened Chocolate
• 1 tablespoon oil

Directions:

1. Lightly grease an 8x8-inch silicone pan.

2. In a food processor, process shredded unsweetened coconut, coconut oil, and Stevia until it forms a dough. Transfer to prepared pan and press on the bottom to form a dough. Place in the freezer to set.

3. Meanwhile, in a microwave-safe Pyrex cup, place chocolate, coconut oil, and Stevia. Heat for 10-second intervals and mix well. Do not overheat, just until you have mixed the mixture thoroughly. Pour over dough.

4. Return to the freezer until set.

5. Serve and enjoy.

Nutrition Info:

• Per Servings 4.0g Carbs, 2.0g Protein, 22.0g Fat, 222 Calories

Coconut Macadamia Nut Bombs

Servings: 4
Cooking Time: 0 Mins

Ingredients:

• 2 packets stevia
• 5 tbsps unsweetened coconut powder
• 10 tbsps coconut oil
• 3 tbsps chopped macadamia nuts
• Salt to taste

Directions:

1. Heat the coconut oil in a pan over medium heat. Add coconut powder, stevia and salt, stirring to combined well; then remove from heat.

2. Spoon mixture into a lined mini muffin pan. Place in the freezer for a few hours.

3. Sprinkle nuts over the mixture before serving.

Nutrition Info:

• Per Servings 0.2g Carbs, 1.1g Protein, 15.2g Fat, 143 Calories

Strawberry Vanilla Extract Smoothie

Servings: 3
Cooking Time: 5 Mins

Ingredients:

• 1 cup almond milk
• 14 frozen strawberries
• 1 1/2 teaspoons stevia
• What you'll need from the store cupboard:
• 1/2 teaspoon vanilla extract

Directions:

1. Place almond milk and strawberries in a blender, blend until creamy. Add vanilla and stevia if desired,

blend again and serve.

Nutrition Info:
- Per Servings 5g Carbs, 12.8g Protein, 18.8g Fat, 240.4 Calories

Boysenberry And Greens Shake

Servings: 1
Cooking Time: 0 Minutes

Ingredients:
- ¼ cup coconut milk
- 2 tbsps Boysenberry
- 2 packets Stevia, or as needed
- ¼ cup Baby Kale salad mix
- 3 tbsps MCT oil
- 1 ½ cups water

Directions:
1. Add all ingredients in a blender.
2. Blend until smooth and creamy.
3. Serve and enjoy.

Nutrition Info:
- Per Servings 3.9g Carbs, 1.7g Protein, 55.1g Fat, 502 Calories

Raspberry-choco Shake

Servings: 1
Cooking Time: 0 Minutes

Ingredients:
- ¼ cup heavy cream, liquid
- 1 tbsp cocoa powder
- 1 packet Stevia, or more to taste
- ¼ cup raspberries
- 1 ½ cups water

Directions:
1. Add all ingredients in a blender.
2. Blend until smooth and creamy.
3. Serve and enjoy.

Nutrition Info:
- Per Servings 11.1g Carbs, 3.8g Protein, 45.0g Fat, 438 Calories

Fast 'n Easy Cookie In A Mug

Servings: 1
Cooking Time: 5 Minutes

Ingredients:
- 1 tablespoon butter
- 3 tablespoons almond flour
- 1 tablespoon erythritol
- 1 egg yolk

- 1/8 teaspoon vanilla extract
- A dash of cinnamon
- A pinch of salt

Directions:
1. Mix all ingredients in a microwave-safe mug.
2. Nuke in the microwave for 3 minutes.
3. Let it rest for a minute.
4. Serve and enjoy.

Nutrition Info:
- Per Servings 1.4g Carbs, 3.5g Protein, 17.8g Fat, 180 Calories

Garden Greens & Yogurt Shake

Servings: 1
Cooking Time: 0 Minutes

Ingredients:
- 1 cup whole milk yogurt
- 1 cup Garden greens
- 3 tbsp MCT oil
- 1 tbsp flaxseed, ground
- 1 cup water
- 1 packet Stevia, or more to taste

Directions:
1. Add all ingredients in a blender.
2. Blend until smooth and creamy.
3. Serve and enjoy.

Nutrition Info:
- Per Servings 7.2g Carbs, 11.7g Protein, 53g Fat, 581 Calories

Coco-loco Creamy Shake

Servings: 1
Cooking Time: 0 Minutes

Ingredients:
- ½ cup coconut milk
- 2 tbsp Dutch-processed cocoa powder, unsweetened
- 1 cup brewed coffee, chilled
- 1 tbsp hemp seeds
- 1-2 packets Stevia
- 3 tbsps MCT oil or coconut oil

Directions:
1. Add all ingredients in a blender.
2. Blend until smooth and creamy.
3. Serve and enjoy.

Nutrition Info:
- Per Servings 10.2g Carbs, 5.4g Protein, 61.1g Fat, 567 Calories

Choco-chia Pudding

Servings: 4
Cooking Time: 5 Minutes

Ingredients:

- ¼ cup fresh or frozen raspberries
- 1 scoop chocolate protein powder
- 1 cup unsweetened almond milk
- 3 tbsp Chia seeds
- 1 tsp Stevia (optional)
- 5 tablespoons coconut oil

Directions:

1. Mix the chocolate protein powder and almond milk.
2. Add the chia seeds and mix well with a whisk or a fork. Add the coconut oil.
3. Flavor with Stevia depending on the desired sweetness.
4. Let it rest for 5 minutes and continue stirring.
5. Serve and enjoy.

Nutrition Info:

- Per Servings 10g Carbs, 11.5g Protein, 19.6g Fat, 243.5 Calories

Creamy Choco Shake

Servings: 1
Cooking Time: 0 Minutes

Ingredients:

- ½ cup heavy cream
- 2 tbsp cocoa powder
- 1 packet Stevia, or more to taste
- 1 cup water
- 3 tbsps coconut oil

Directions:

1. Add all ingredients in a blender.
2. Blend until smooth and creamy.
3. Serve and enjoy.

Nutrition Info:

- Per Servings 7.9g Carbs, 3.2g Protein, 64.6g Fat, 582 Calories

Spicy Cheese Crackers

Servings: 4
Cooking Time: 10 Mins

Ingredients:

- 3/4 cup almond flour
- 1 egg
- 2 tablespoons cream cheese
- 2 cups shredded Parmesan cheese
- 1/2 teaspoon red pepper flakes
- 1 tablespoon dry ranch salad dressing mix

Directions:

1. Preheat oven to 425 degrees F.
2. Combine Parmesan and cream cheese in a microwave safe bowl and microwave in 30 second intervals. Add the cheese to mix well, and whisk along the almond flour, egg, ranch seasoning, and red pepper flakes, stirring occasionally.
3. Transfer the dough in between two parchment-lined baking sheets. Form the dough into rolls by cutting off plum-sized pieces of dough with dough cutter into 1-inch square pieces, yielding about 60 pieces.
4. Place crackers to a baking sheet lined parchment. Bake for 5 minutes, flipping halfway, then continue to bake for 5 minutes more. Chill before serving.

Nutrition Info:

- Per Servings 18g Carbs, 17g Protein, 4g Fat, 235 Calories

Date: _____

MY SHOPPING LIST

Recipe

From the kicthen of ....

Serves .... Prep time .... Cook time ....

☐ Difficulty   ☐ Easy   ☐ Medium   ☐ Hard

Ingredient

Yummy!

Directions

Appendix A : Measurement Conversions

BASIC KITCHEN CONVERSIONS & EQUIVALENTS

DRY MEASUREMENTS CONVERSION CHART

3 TEASPOONS = 1 TABLESPOON = 1/16 CUP

6 TEASPOONS = 2 TABLESPOONS = 1/8 CUP

12 TEASPOONS = 4 TABLESPOONS = 1/4 CUP

24 TEASPOONS = 8 TABLESPOONS = 1/2 CUP

36 TEASPOONS = 12 TABLESPOONS = 3/4 CUP

48 TEASPOONS = 16 TABLESPOONS = 1 CUP

METRIC TO US COOKING CONVERSIONS

OVEN TEMPERATURES

120 °C = 250 °F

160 °C = 320 °F

180° C = 350 °F

205 °C = 400 °F

220 °C = 425 °F

LIQUID MEASUREMENTS CONVERSION CHART

8 FLUID OUNCES = 1 CUP = 1/2 PINT = 1/4 QUART

16 FLUID OUNCES = 2 CUPS = 1 PINT = 1/2 QUART

32 FLUID OUNCES = 4 CUPS = 2 PINTS = 1 QUART

 = 1/4 GALLON

128 FLUID OUNCES = 16 CUPS = 8 PINTS = 4 QUARTS = 1 GALLON

BAKING IN GRAMS

1 CUP FLOUR = 140 GRAMS

1 CUP SUGAR = 150 GRAMS

1 CUP POWDERED SUGAR = 160 GRAMS

1 CUP HEAVY CREAM = 235 GRAMS

VOLUME

1 MILLILITER = 1/5 TEASPOON

5 ML = 1 TEASPOON

15 ML = 1 TABLESPOON

240 ML = 1 CUP OR 8 FLUID OUNCES

1 LITER = 34 FL. OUNCES

US TO METRIC COOKING CONVERSIONS

1/5 TSP = 1 ML

1 TSP = 5 ML

1 TBSP = 15 ML

1 FL OUNCE = 30 ML

1 CUP = 237 ML

1 PINT (2 CUPS) = 473 ML

1 QUART (4 CUPS) = .95 LITER

1 GALLON (16 CUPS) = 3.8 LITERS

1 OZ = 28 GRAMS

1 POUND = 454 GRAMS

BUTTER

1 CUP BUTTER = 2 STICKS = 8 OUNCES = 230 GRAMS = 8 TABLESPOONS

WHAT DOES 1 CUP EQUAL

1 CUP = 8 FLUID OUNCES

1 CUP = 16 TABLESPOONS

1 CUP = 48 TEASPOONS

1 CUP = 1/2 PINT

1 CUP = 1/4 QUART

1 CUP = 1/16 GALLON

1 CUP = 240 ML

WEIGHT

1 GRAM = .035 OUNCES

100 GRAMS = 3.5 OUNCES

500 GRAMS = 1.1 POUNDS

1 KILOGRAM = 35 OUNCES

BAKING PAN CONVERSIONS

1 CUP ALL-PURPOSE FLOUR = 4.5 OZ

1 CUP ROLLED OATS = 3 OZ 1 LARGE EGG = 1.7 OZ

1 CUP BUTTER = 8 OZ 1 CUP MILK = 8 OZ

1 CUP HEAVY CREAM = 8.4 OZ

1 CUP GRANULATED SUGAR = 7.1 OZ

1 CUP PACKED BROWN SUGAR = 7.75 OZ

1 CUP VEGETABLE OIL = 7.7 OZ

1 CUP UNSIFTED POWDERED SUGAR = 4.4 OZ

BAKING PAN CONVERSIONS

9-INCH ROUND CAKE PAN = 12 CUPS

10-INCH TUBE PAN =16 CUPS

11-INCH BUNDT PAN = 12 CUPS

9-INCH SPRINGFORM PAN = 10 CUPS

9 X 5 INCH LOAF PAN = 8 CUPS

9-INCH SQUARE PAN = 8 CUPS

Appendix B : Recipes Index

Made in the USA
Las Vegas, NV
24 February 2024